RIDE IT!

The

Complete

Book

of

ENDURANCE RACING

ISBN 0 85429 253 5

© John Robinson 1979

First published August 1979

A FOULIS Motorcycling Book

Printed and bound in England by the publishers:
Haynes Publishing Group
Sparkford, Yeovil, Somerset BA22 7JJ, England

Distributed in North America by:
Haynes Publications Inc
861 Lawrence Drive, Newbury Park, California 91320,
USA
Editor **Jeff Clew**
Cover design **Phill Jennings**
Layout Design **John Rose**

RIDE IT!

The Complete Book of

ENDURANCE RACING

John Robinson

Contents

7

Acknowledgements

There are many factors interwoven to make up the world of long-distance racing, each with its own history, development and technical details. I am very grateful to the numerous, enthusiastic individuals who supplied specific data as well as background information.

The following people and companies unhesitatingly spared their own time and made valuable material available, and deserve particular thanks:

Moto Revue magazine, especially Bruno Nardini and Philippe Michel; Gerald Davison and the Honda Britain race team; John Cowie; Steve Thrush and David Lamb of Dunlop; Dave Degens of Dresda Autos; the UK staff at Michelin.

Photographs were supplied by Rod Sloane, Don Morley (All-Sport Photographic), Dave Walker, Honda UK and *Motorcycle Mechanics* magazine.

Introduction

Long distance racing is a subtle blend of all the characteristics which make motorcycle competition so attractive. It has the speed, the power and the sheer atmosphere of the grands prix. At the same time the machinery is mainly based on roadster models. The spectators can identify with machines actually being raced and the race hardware is easily available, at far less than the horrifying cost associated with pure racers. It is partly the cost which makes GP machines so exclusive and which set F750 on the road to general disdain — something which also threatened F1.

Racing is never cheap but the wealth of a rider or sponsor is less likely to buy success in Endurance events. Competition at this level also sets stamina and reliability against the increasing fragility of higher performance. The races lasting for 24 hours — and even the shorter 6- and 8-hour events — are a great leveller of both men and machines. It is the same for everyone and this equality, this classless democracy, has an attraction which most motorcyclists find easy to appreciate. When you're riding through a hundred miles of rain, your position in society will not keep you dry ...

Development of endurance racers tends to go hand-in-hand with roadsters and the general climate of motorcycling. If it can offer the best of the racing and the roadster worlds, there have also been depressed times when it has reflected the worst of each. But the general freedom of the long distance racer — the lack of formality, regulations and red tape — tends to provide a stimulus for further development and, at the same time, to keep it the friendliest of motorised sports.

Roadsters stand to benefit more directly from Endurance racing; as new developments proceed on the track, the next generation of roadsters can be seen unfolding. And as roadsters improve, the endurance racers are given better raw material. Bultaco, Ossa, Montesa, Triumph, Ducati, Moto Guzzi, BMW, Laverda and Honda have all taken advantage of this re-cycling development — and its attendant publicity. Ironically, Kawasaki, whose machines had a major effect on the sport, tended to keep their distance.

As well as prototype machines finding their way into production, detail improvements, such as tyres, suspension and chains have also filtered through to the roadster.

The racing (and some of the racers) is conducted in a slightly eccentric manner but perhaps the appeal of Endurance racing lies in paradox. That small machines can keep up the pace of more powerful devices; that roadsters can compete with racers; that the speed of a grand prix can be maintained for up to 24 hours.

It also makes a fascinating alternative to the strictly-governed grand prix classes. In addition to the skill and finesse associated with first-rate racing, the Endurance machines have an element of brute force. They are the only racers today which equate with the supercharged pre-war machines or the alcohol-burning Brooklands monsters of the same era. In those glorious days the riders could use their machines — in differing states of tune — for quarter-mile sprints, three-lap races, 100- and 200- mile events through to 'normal' road races and long-distance, record-breaking sessions.

That was their level of freedom and today's Endurance racers are, in a sense, keeping our options open.

Chapter One
All racing is endurance

A line of blue-uniformed police, shoulder to shoulder, hustle spectators off the track and back into the enclosure; the last photographers are chased to the safety of the Armco barriers; sixty riders line up opposite their machines, nervously ignoring one another and fiddling with their gloves and visors with exaggerated concentration.

The flag drops and the riders sprint to their bikes, trying too hard to fire up the big engines, then curving out onto the start straight, weaving to avoid other riders. Occasionally a bike rears up on its back wheel as the 120 horsepower engine suddenly gets into its power band. As the noise in the pit straight builds up to an intimidating level, the first riders are disappearing into the first turn and taking chances with the still-cold slick tyres. They are racing, as hard as in any Grand Prix, for the prestige and the psychological advantage of an early lead. As the last stragglers leave the pits with spluttering, gassed-up engines, a formation of jet aircraft swoops low across the grandstands, adding twined columns of red and blue smoke to the heat haze. Mechanics get back to their pit counters and the first bikes thunder into view, a dozen of them close together, their exhausts drowning the cheers of the crowd.

Despite the pace of the bikes, the anticipation and elation of the onlookers, each one of the riders is hoping that he will still be up in front when the flag drops again, 24 hours later.

This is endurance racing. Not a battle against the clock. No longer a game of tactics but a race to the finish and one in which the first laps are as important as the last ones. The chequered flag will fall across the finishing line 24 hours later and the team that then crosses the line with the most laps to its credit is the winner.

And that is the real difference between this and a Grand Prix race: the pace is similar, the racing as close, but instead of one rider standing on the winner's rostrum there will be two, backed up by a pit crew whose performance is as crucial as that of the riders. The machines, too, are different from GP racers. They are more varied, for a start. So varied in fact, that one or two of them will be actual GP machines, with lights added and one or two

The start of the 1978 24-hour race at Spa
(photo by Motorcycle Mechanics)

Early days at Thruxton – the works-prepared Royal Enfield twin was a rare sight on race tracks
(photo by Motorcycle Mechanics)

less obvious modifications. They will vary in size from 350 cc up to 1200 cc and, in performance, from virtually standard roadsters to machines with engines rated at 130 horsepower or more.

Not all the races last for 24 hours. One season might include a dozen events, three or four of which will occupy a full day and night. Others have a limit of twelve, eight or six hours, or may run on a distance basis, usually 1,000 km. The shorter the race, the more hectic it gets.

The big differences in the size and performance of the machines are not so important as they might seem. The length of time and distance usually proves to be a great equaliser, not only between machines but between privateer and factory as well.

It has been argued that, for short-circuit racing, the ideal machine is one which crosses the finishing line (preferably before anything else) and then proceeds to blow up in an orderly manner. That would demonstrate that each component was giving the absolute maximum. It isn't easy to stretch that philosophy over a period of 24 hours, especially as the machines have to accommodate a fair amount of servicing and maintenance during the race itself.

All forms of racing are a balance between speed and endurance. The further you go back in time, the more the endurance aspect takes precedence. Early events were usually held from place to place, on public roads. The first recorded race, according to the Guinness Book of Records, was from Paris to Dieppe, in 1897. Some of these runs became particularly popular in both Europe and America, but the condition of the 'roads' and the state of machine development meant that uncertainty ruled over speed.

Circular routes, such as the closed circuit used at the Parc des Princes, Paris, in 1903, had obvious attractions and, in forming the basis of today's racing, also caused a decisive parting of the ways. At one extreme the wooden boarded, oval tracks became the fore-runners of the purpose-built stadium and the highly specialised forms of sport such as speedway.

At the other extreme, road circuits gave rise to road racing. The very short oval tracks demanded special machinery; designed purely for speed, the bikes were stripped down, functional, and as light and fast as possible. Reliability could, for the duration of the short races, take second place to horsepower. Meanwhile, road racing demanded other things: reliability, manoeuvrability and, eventually, handling and braking were as important as the ability to go quickly. Each advance in engine design called for an equivalent improvement throughout the whole machine.

Events like the Isle of Man Tourist Trophy began, as the name suggests, as a reliability trial for roadsters (originally for cars; later with an easier, 15.81 mile, course for motorcycles, in 1907). Here, manufacturers could prove the worth of their vehicles and two more aspects of racing were introduced: the test of a machine (as opposed to its rider) and commercial pressure.

When reliability was good enough to allow performance to be exploited, more specialised 'racing' models were developed. Eventually these roadster-based racers were used on short, closed circuits of the Brooklands style and short circuit racing evolved from there.

There are many outside pressures on racing. Manufacturers see it as valuable publicity with which to promote their roadsters. Circuit owners want a spectacle to satisfy the paying public. Organising bodies are anxious to achieve maximum safety and a good name for the sport, and so on. The result, in nearly every branch of racing, is 'The Formula'. Whether this is good or bad depends on how it is devised and what you want from the racing. In its most restrictive form it ensures that all machines are pretty well identical — as in the Honda 125

The early Triumph and BSA threes took over from the parallel twins in production racing. Malcolm Uphill rides one of the drum-braked models at Thruxton
(photo by Motorcycle Mechanics)

All racing is endurance

races or in speedway – and it should provide close racing with the best *rider*, not machine, emerging as the winner. The drawback to this kind of formula is that it inhibits development and innovation.

The formula can also be a bad thing if it is not applied wisely. Devised to control racing or to ensure fair play, it can also strangle the sport or, at best, make it excessively complicated. And, as every production racer knows, the more rules there are, the easier it is to find loopholes.

Capacity classes and formulae have gradually been removed from endurance racing and have allowed the sport to flourish. This is possibly because this type of racing doesn't have enormous spectator appeal, nor does it have an individual person as a winner. The successful races have catered for the spectator by turning themselves into carnivals, while the machines and the race teams receive as much attention as the riders. It wasn't always that way. Early long-distance races were regarded as a feat of endurance on the part of the rider. And to ensure this, there was only one rider per machine!

In the period up to 1914 there were many road trials, leading, because of the state of the 'roads', to events like

As the Tridents proved more and more versatile they were turned into successful racers, paving the way for F750. Works rider Percy Tait is seen here on the most famous triple – 'Slippery Sam'

(photo by Motorcycle Mechanics)

the Scott Trial. This was deliberately devised, each year, with the express intention of its being too difficult for anyone to finish – yet someone invariably did! This opened the way for purely off-road events and the same sort of pioneer spirit exists now in off-road sport, such as the six-day trials and the American Baja 1000, all with one rider per bike and the minimum of outside support. Riders in these events, using only a couple of hand tools, can fix a punctured tyre very nearly as quickly as the slick pit crews at Le Mans. Manufacturers also got into the habit of setting time and distance endurance records.

The mechanised aspects of World War I gave many of its survivors a wider and deeper understanding of mechanical things. In the post-war period, specific racing designs appeared and long-distance races – of 100 to 300 miles – were organised. Ensurance events still referred to the endurance of the rider, apart from the publicity-orientated record attempts which would employ relays of riders. Events on road circuits, such as the Bol d'Or were established and quickly gained popularity, especially when the industry saw the advertising potential and started to support them. Other reliability tests, such as the Maudes Trophy and long-distance runs like the American coast-to-coast or Three Flags (Canada-Mexico) also enjoyed a fair amount of prestige.

In motorcycling there are hardly any 'new' ideas; very few things were not at least thought about before 1914. What is new, though, is the ability to make them *work* as new materials and processes are evolved. Developments

in World War II brought huge advances in metallurgy, for example, which would have a large effect on motorcycle engineering. But, in post-war Europe, only cheap, utilitarian transport was needed. Racing, particularly on the Continent, survived on a diet of cheap lightweights and rehashed pre-war designs. Together with a ban on superchargers and the restriction to low octane fuel, this meant that race speeds in the late '40s were roughly the same as those achieved in 1935.

But alloy engines, gas-oil suspension, rear swinging arms and other changes were all on the way. The UK concentrated on short-circuit racing and, of course, the TT. In Europe there was more lightweight racing, organised on a local level, plus long-distance races. These were also dominated by lightweights, 125s and 175s, with the occasional incursion of a BMW or a Manx Norton.

The '50s saw the domination of the Manx singles, with the Italian Gilera, Guzzi, Mondial and MV at GP level. Production-type racing was at an all-time low. The Bol d'Or was eventually suspended through lack of interest.

However, the growing Spanish industry, makers of lightweights and enthusiasts for road racing, saw a way to do what they liked doing and get publicity for it. The Barcelona 24-hour race, held on closed public roads at Montjuich Park, was engineered to allow factory prototypes. This brightened things up considerably, just as the Japanese were about to liven up Grand Prix lightweight racing.

In British production machine events, the Gold Star BSA was giving way to Triumph and Norton twins. In '61 a 250 Honda won the 250 class at the Thruxton 500-miler, but in big bike development Norton's Domi-racer, a pushrod twin, was about all there was. Developments in GP racing revitalised the sporting world and had spin-offs which helped the roadster machines for some time to come. The Japanese pulled out of road racing and the FIM tightened up its formulae, restricting the number of cylinders and gears in the GP classes. In 1969 production racers were not allowed to have double overhead camshafts or disc valves — features which were to appear on many totally standard machines.

From '68 onwards there were several developments in quick succession which had a direct bearing on endurance racing. The Trident and CB750 announced the beginning of the 'superbike' era. Dunlop produced their K81 tyre as a direct result of their participation in GP racing. The newly revived Bol d'Or placed less emphasis on capacity classes and the 'prototype' class usually meant anything with two wheels. A Formula 750 was drawn up which put UK racing on a par with American racing, allowed Triumph to build 'standard' Tridents that did about 150 mph, and injected more excitement into short-circuit racing. This eventually led to a World Championship and, more immediately, the Trans-Atlantic series of team races.

Bearing in mind the outside pressures which bear on racing, it isn't surprising to learn that one of the people who drafted the initial F750 was involved with Motor Circuit Developments (who own Brands Hatch) and another worked for Triumph.

200-mile races like those at Daytona and at Imola caught the public's imagination and the manufacturers' interest. The modified roadsters used in these events also made good prototypes for the endurance races and formed the basis for race kits which could be used to uprate stock bikes.

The European response was pretty healthy as well. Factories like Ducati, Laverda, BMW and Guzzi raced their own machines and the roadsters they sold were also suitable for conversion into endurance racers. The climate was about as healthy as it could be. Continental organisers, aware that 24-hour races did not have the spectator-appeal of a GP, made use of the carnival atmosphere which went with places like Le Mans, turning

One of the first Japanese machines to make itself in production and long-distance races — the 500 Suzuki, ridden here by Martyn Ashwood. Stan Woods and Jean-Claude Chemarin also used the two-stroke twins earlier in their endurance racing careers

(photo by Motorcycle Mechanics)

the events into a weekend of entertainment. The Japanese factories, which had no official racing commitments, started to take an interest with semi-official racing entries via importers and dealers. The racing itself generated specialists who built bikes specifically for this kind of event. Eventually Honda set up a fully committed race programme. All these factors combined to build endurance racing into the big business it is today.

The concept of endurance racing has changed very little since the early days. The biggest difference is the shift in emphasis — away from the endurance 'feat' of the rider and towards the concept of the machine as a focal point backed up by a team of people. And now there is less emphasis on *endurance* and more on *racing*. With the bare minimum of regulations, the events have been able to change with the times. Mechanical developments and the progress made by the race teams have produced machines which are reliable enough to be *raced* for 24 hours. In itself, this is quite an achievement. It has brought endurance racing to a peak and any logical development ought now to bring back the *endurance* aspect. One way would be to make the races harder still and a 30-hour race, with teams of five riders, is being planned in America. The alternative is to apply 'The Formula'. This, with the prospect of a World Championship, seems to be the favourite and could easily remove much of the interest from long-distance racing.

The point where endurance racing really took off was right at the end of the '60s. Motorcycling enjoyed one of its periodic booms; specialists like Dresda and Japauto were using production engines to make purpose-built racers and new, bigger machines were on the way.

Because the racing wasn't tied by any formula, the teams could take advantage of any new developments as they came along. The more powerful machines needed better brakes, and brakes which would last a reasonable

Opposite top **The production TT was run on a class handicap basis, giving the 250s a fair chance against the bigger bikes. Chas Mortimer chose a 250 Yamaha and, a couple of years later, made an appearance on a four-cylinder Suzuki endurance racer at Nurburgring**
Opposite bottom **The style of production racing in the TT, which evolved into the Formula One Championship, encouraged European manufacturers to return to racing. Keith Martin rode a six-cylinder 750 Benelli prepared by Agrati Sales**
Agrati Sales
Below **Sheer speed made the three-cylinder 500 Kawasaki an attractive choice for production-based events. Terry Grotefeld throws the MCM Kawasaki through Montjuich Park's winding curves in the 1972 Barcelona 24-hour race**
(photos by Motorcycle Mechanics)

All racing is endurance

length of time; Dresda were using an eight-leading-shoe brake when hydraulic discs first became available. Then they needed better tyres — which Dunlop provided — and then frames which gave better handling. All these things came as a matter of course and were soon adopted by the racers. When the 750s became 900s there was no capacity restriction to stop them, merely a 1-litre ceiling. Even this was lifted to 1200 cc for the Bol d'Or, anticipating the arrival of bikes like the CBX Honda and the XS1100 Yamaha by nearly a year.

The races themselves are as varied as the bikes. They

Dave Croxford on one of the John Player Nortons. Norton certainly tried hard enough with their pushrod twins but were outpaced in F750 and endurance events *(photo by Motorcycle Mechanics)*

can cover a distance varying from 1,000 km to around 4,000 km, spanning times from six hours to a full 24. The circuits go to similar extremes, from purpose-built tracks, like Le Mans and Paul Ricard, to circuits using public roads such as Montjuich Park or the long, very fast Belgian circuit at Spa-Francorchamps. In between there is a wide variety, each with its own peculiarities and demands: Rouen, Mettet, Zandvoort, Mugello, Nürburgring. In fact, one of the biggest feats of endurance for many of the teams is the trek back and forth across Europe, just to get to the races. In June '78 there was a 24-hour race at Spa on the 3rd and 4th, the Italian round at Misano on the 11th and an 8-hour race at the Nürburgring, Germany on the 18th. All three counted for the *Coupe d'Endurance* and for many teams it was hardly worth returning home in between races — as soon as they got there, they had to set out for the next one.

Chapter Two
Development

A large part of endurance racing's appeal is that it remains a real sport, in spite of the high costs and the handsome prizes. Many of the competitors obviously find it satisfying enough merely to take part. For the spectators, there is a similar interest in the vast range of machinery. There are not many places where you could see an OW31 Yamaha competing against works Hondas, an almost standard, shaft-drive XS1100 Yamaha, and an American team on a Yoshimura Suzuki. These machines appeared at the 1978 Bol d'Or, along with an experimental, watercooled V-6 Laverda, assorted Kawasakis, BMWs, Guzzis, Ducatis and outright hybrid specials.

If the spectator got bored he could turn to a motocross, a museum, trials demonstrations and a trials course where he could take part himself. For further amusement there were air displays, stunt car drivers, film shows and even a bull ring.

It is this unique blend of racing and carnival side-attractions that has made endurance racing a commercial

Endurance racing opened the door to all-comers ... an MV powers out of la Source hairpin in Belgium's 24-hour race *(photo by Motorcycle Mechanics)*

success. There is something for everyone: competitor, spectator, organiser and sponsor.

At a time when Grand Prix racing seems to be getting further removed from roadster machines, endurance events are a direct demonstration of racing improving the breed. It takes us back to an era when racers were recognisably based on models that anyone could buy.

Of course, it's easy to confuse 'development' with publicity — and it's in the interests of some parties to do so. But, having built and tested components to his own satisfaction, a manufacturer can use the race-track to show them off. In many ways, racing conditions are ideal for engines: they run at optimum temperatures; they are ridden by experts; and they don't have to last more than a few thousand miles. The real enemies of any machine are cold starts, short journeys and the effects of time — lack of maintenance, corrosion and fatigue.

So the race-track is often a *good* place to demonstrate new machines; but it means proving their worth publicly, in an atmosphere where the winner takes all and there are no consolation prizes. It's this atmosphere which counts — the factories are forced to gamble on their product and expertise in the harsh and unflattering light of publicity.

A manufacturer is also tied to what he already sells. Any radical departure might suggest that his marketed designs were less than perfect. The Godier-Genoud team were able to transform endurance racing with their redesigned Kawasaki specials. They did it by careful consideration of what was available and what it then needed to be successful. The 903 cc Kawasaki was the best engine they could get for the job. They modified it to get the necessary level of power without spoiling reliability. The really radical change was to make the engine an integral part of a race machine — with a totally new chassis designed as much for improved access and reliability as for better speed and handling.

The team was given semi-official help via SIDEMM, the importer of Kawasaki machines. It would have been less easy for Kawasaki themselves to have built such machines, amounting to a formal admission that their big bikes were heavy and didn't handle as well as they might. It's possible that the Godier-Genoud frames wouldn't have been suitable for production anyway, purely on a cost basis — racing *doesn't* improve the breed, as far as production engineers are concerned.

When Honda got into endurance racing, on a much more official level, they had to feature designs which were either used on existing machines or would appear on future Honda roadsters. That much was part of the design team's brief.

Exotic engine parts were acceptable to some degree — indeed the race-going public expect special alloys, trick camshafts and noisy exhausts. But the chassis and cycle parts remained uncompromisingly orthodox. Honda either believed that a conventional frame was the best available or could not change it without letting the world see that they could build something better than they put into their roadsters.

Obviously there were many detail changes. They had to make conventional suspension and transmission work under racing conditions — and they did. More than that, the wheels, chains and dampers used on the racers appeared on production bikes within a matter of months.

This generation of Hondas, the six-cylinder CBX and a new range of four-cylinder machines, were among the best roadsters ever built. But that doesn't mean there isn't a better way. The bigger, more powerful bikes suffered problems with chain wear and handling — Honda put their not inconsiderable effort into curing the symptoms and were successful.

In a pure racing effort, such as Formula One car racing, such a situation would be intolerable. For example, the problems with chains were firstly, the wear rate and, secondly, the effects of transmission loads on the frame and suspension. Development to cure this might follow the lines adopted by the special-builders, like Mike Tomkinson with his highly original chassis and suspension. Privateers like this can happily explore the unknown but if established manufacturers tried the same thing — in public — they would be risking more than their reputation. Better not to venture; unless, of course, one of the specials started beating them ...

Honda have experimented with linked brakes and anti-dive suspension but, out on the race-track, development is restricted to detail changes. The real value of any development work is in the failures — once you have eliminated all the ideas and components which don't work, you are left with the ones which do.

At least endurance racing leaves the teams fairly free to develop machines in whichever way they choose. The arbitrary rules governing other types of racing are often out-dated by new developments. Even capacity classes are subjected to this when, for instance, two-strokes start to outpace the four-strokes. Then you have the complicated nonsense of one 'size' of two-stroke versus another 'size' of four-stroke. The only thing they have in common is that they are supposed to be equally competitive. Nothing is new, though — the same 'formula' was applied in 1911 when Scott two-strokes started beating the four-stroke machines. This was carefully devised so that an air-cooled two-stroke had its displacement multiplied by a factor of 1·25 in order to calculate its official capacity. A liquid-cooled two-stroke was subject to an increase of 1·32. Apart from the Scott, the horizon was remarkably clear of liquid-cooled two-strokes and the 'fairness' factor was put to good use in Alfred Scott's advertising material.

It was around this time that the first endurance events were evolving. One of the UK's favourite runs,

Land's End to John O'Groats, was covered in 41 hours 30 minutes, during 1908.

Long-distance races were popular in America, too. In 1912 an 8 hp Harley-Davidson averaged 49·43 mph for seven hours to win a race at San José. Unlike European events, two riders per machine were allowed. The following year Harleys scored a 1–2–3 in a 225-mile road race from Harrisburg to Philadelphia, Pennsylvania and back.

Dirt track ovals were springing up, and in 1914 the two types of racing were combined at Dodge City when a 300-mile race was organised on a 2-mile dirt track. Specialised racers were already appearing – one of the fastest bikes in the world was the 1912 Indian twin which had four-valve heads and a top speed approaching 100 mph. One set a record for the flying kilometre at 93·48 mph – but they were also used in long-distance races such as the 300-mile event at Savannah, Georgia, held over an 11·5 mile circuit. Another race, in the streets of Venice, California offered a $2,000 prize. That must have been a fairly substantial prize in 1914 but the levels of performance were no less impressive. In 1915 a Harley-Davidson averaged 89·11 mph for 100 miles on a wooden-board track at Chicago.

Harley's race-model for 1916 was called the model 17 and featured four-valve, pentroof heads. For short

UK production racing had always veered towards what is now Formula One. Charlie Williams, on a Yoshimura Honda holds off a Desmo Ducati and the Gus Kuhn Norton ridden by Dave Potter

(photo by Motorcycle Mechanics)

track work the engine was mounted in a very low, rigid frame while sprung front forks were fitted for long-distance races. By this time there were regular races lasting from 150 to 300 miles, plus several 24-hour endurance runs and 450-mile events which went on past nightfall. The sheer size of North America lent itself to epic record-breaking runs such as the 1,685 mile Three Flags trip from Canada to Mexico. Other favourites were the 1,244 miles of mainly dirt roads from Denver to Chicago and, of course the coast-to-coast marathon.

By this time endurance events had been well-established in Sweden – the Novemberkasan being described as their 'oldest and most demanding trial', which Husqvarna won in 1916, covering 475 km in less than 20 hours. Another event, the Swedish May Cup, covered 1,700 km from Stockholm–Malmö–Gothenburg and back to Stockholm. It was a race but the endurance aspect is brought out in a letter to Husqvarna from Einar

Development

Sundström, talking about his Moto-Reve-powered Husqvarna: '...the engine ran without a falter for the first part of the race, including a non-stop period of 36 hours before the first obligatory rest period...' By 1922 the May Cup had been toughened up – to cover a course of 2,100 km.

Meanwhile, in America, typical professionalism had entered the proceedings. Machine preparation was painstaking in its attention to detail. For example, nuts and bolts were taped, wired, shellacked or even soldered into place. Quick-fill tanks were used, the Indian team having pressurised dump tanks for oil and fuel while Harley-Davidson used six-inch diameter injectors to re-fill oil tanks. The Harley team was pretty well organised – the riders were equipped with English cricket gloves to protect their hands from flying stones, and a clean pair of goggles was kept in the pits for each rider, ready adjusted to his head size. A look-out on the course had a telephone link with the pits to warn them of incoming machines, and the bikes featured QD wheels and quick-release brake anchors, enabling the mechanics to complete a

Continental racing had moved in a similar direction with purpose-built endurance specials like this Swiss-entered Gold Wing *(photo by Motorcycle Mechanics)*

wheel change in 40 seconds.

What was to become the most famous long-distance race of all was launched in France, in 1922. With 28 entries in its first year, the Bol d'Or 24-hour race was to grow into one of France's most prestigious meetings.

Racing in England was epitomised by Brooklands and the TT, where the arduous nature of the course demanded the stamina and reliability of the endurance racer combined with the performance of the short-circuit speedster. Long-distance runs were attempted on a record-breaking basis, either on public roads or on closed circuits. The Maudes Trophy, awarded by an ACU committee, was presented not solely for endurance feats but for the year's most notable achievement. Naturally most of these achievements concentrated on a combination of speed and reliability. In 1923, Norton took the world 12-hour record at Brooklands and gained the Maudes Trophy with it. They kept the trophy the next year by running a sidecar outfit 4,088 miles in eighteen days.

In 1929 a 348 cc Dunelt was awarded the Maudes Trophy for covering an amazing 25,000 miles in 23 days at Montlhéry. Records have always had an appeal of their own, although, without detailed knowledge of the circumstances, it is difficult to see them in a true perspective. In 1937, Fred Ham rode for 1,825 miles in 24 hours at Muroc Dry Lake. (The previous record had been set by

Gnôme et Rhône at Montlhéry — using a team of *four* riders). In the same year, Tabard won the Bol d'Or at Montlhéry on a 500 Norton, covering 1,899 km (1,177 miles); like Ham, Tabard had no co-rider.

During the '30s American racing became rationalised, the distance events crystallising into 200-milers which were to form the backbone of American road racing. The Savannah 200-mile race was switched to Daytona in 1936, where it remained and became America's prestige event.

In the years following World War II, British manufacturers made use of long-distance achievements as a means of gaining publicity for new models. When Triumph announced their 650 Thunderbird in 1949 they rode three machines to Montlhéry where each covered 500 high-speed miles before being ridden home again. Running on 72-octane petrol they averaged just over 90 mph at the circuit, and each put in timed laps at over 100 mph. A 500 Velocette became the first machine to average more than 100 mph for 24 hours — again at Montlhéry.

BSA tried a different approach in 1952. Three A7 twins were ridden over 3,000 miles to take part in the International Six Days Trials, where all three won Gold Medals, and for this achievement the team was awarded the Maudes Trophy. More recently manufacturers have

resorted to pure endurance attempts. Honda ran a team of 50 cc machines for seven days and nights at Goodwood. Some years later BMW took two of their motorcycles to the Isle of Man for a similar, non-stop, week of high-speed riding. Suzuki chose a route which followed the UK coastline.

Long-distance racing finally came to Britain in 1955 when a 9-hour race was held on the airfield circuit at Thruxton. The first year it was won by a 500 cc BSA Gold Star, while 350 cc Gold Stars took the next two events.

It became a 500-mile race in 1958 and that year the race went to a 650 Triumph shared by Mike Hailwood and Dan Shorey. A Royal Enfield Constellation came second, the best placing this firm were to achieve despite many attempts at this race with their vertical twins ridden by Bob McIntyre.

In '59 a 250 class was included and the overall victory went to the Daniels/Lewis BMW; this machine also won the 24-hour race at Barcelona, ridden by Daniels and Darvill. The Spanish race, also started in the mid-50s, had a prototype class and during this period

London dealer Vincent Davey moved from Nortons to BMWs. Rider John Cowie is seen at the '76 Bol d'Or on the Kuhn BMW   *(photo by Motorcycle Mechanics)*

Development

was pretty well overrun by factory lightweights. The BMW was chased home by three 125s and, the following year, a works 600 BMW was beaten by a 175 Ducati.

The vertical twins still dominated British production racing, although not always receiving the chequered flag. At the 1960 500-miler it was a 650 AJS which managed to beat the more likely Triumph and Norton twins. A slightly longer race – 1,000 km – was held at Silverstone but, with a final switch to Oulton Park, the event only lasted until 1963. Production racing has never held much spectator appeal and long races, without the stimulation of factory support, prototype classes and sufficient side attractions, do not get a big enough crowd to pay their way. Nevertheless the 500-miler managed to get along during the '60s when even the Bol d'Or was suspended through lack of support. In '61 Thruxton race was won by a 650 Triumph and a Honda won the 250 class, against the Ariel two-stroke twins.

Phil Read and Brian Setchell won the event for the next two years, on a Syd Lawton 650 Norton. The racing

Endurance events offered few restrictions. The Italian Benelli factory prepared this device, based on the six-cylinder roadster, for the '77 Bol d'Or

(photo by Rod Sloane)

was certainly attracting the star riders of the time and, since then, virtually all the well-known UK racers have ridden at the 500-miler. Even people who had no involvement in production racing and a distinct preference for GP-style events have made at least one appearance at the UK's longest race. But this wasn't enough to attract more than the hard-core enthusiasts to watch the event and the attendance figures were never very encouraging. The problem was that the racing didn't provide the excitement of ordinary short-circuit events, with a programme of a dozen or so lively races. In those events it was easy to follow the progress of all the riders – if they were in front of someone on the track they were in front in the race, but this didn't apply to long-distance events where two riders could be side by side on the track yet several laps apart in racing positions.

The facilities at Thruxton didn't help, either. The amenities were pretty basic even by the standard of UK circuits. The lap scoreboards and PA system failed to relay any information other than who was actually in the lead. The only supporting attraction would be a couple of hot-dog stalls and this, combined with the English climate and the circuit location – good for an airfield, rather exposed for anything else – acted as an efficient deterrent to many potential spectators.

This was the era of the production machine even in ordinary 500 cc racing. Not surprisingly, 500s and 600s dominated the Thruxton race right through to 1971. The Lawton Norton made it a hat-trick in 1964, and for the next two years 650 Triumphs prepared by the same dealer won the race. Dave Degens, who was riding his own Dresda Triumphs in the continental events, rode Lawton's Triumphs at Thruxton. In 1967 the race was taken by a works 650 Triumph shared by factory tester Percy Tait and Rodney Gould, who was to become 250 World Champion in 1970. The English factories were taking an interest in the production events (races at the TT and mainland internationals would be added to the 500-miler) and the Thruxton name was given to their successful models or components. There were 'Thruxton' camshafts, 'Thruxton' silencers, and Velocette produced a Clubman's version of their 500 single also called 'Thruxton'.

1968 was notable for the win by a 500 Boyer Triumph, the dealer-entered machine taking the lead as the bigger bikes blew up. This was the first 500 to win the event since a BSA Gold Star won the very first, 9-hour race.

The Japanese hadn't started to produce any big machines until then but the rapid Suzuki 250 and 500 cc two-stroke twins were making their presence felt, taking

Bernie Toleman shared this Peckett and McNab Kawasaki with John Cowie, becoming the UK's best-scoring privateers in the endurance series
(photo by Motorcycle Mechanics)

class wins.

In 1969, several things happened which permanently changed the face of endurance racing. Triumph and BSA launched their three-cylinder 750s, the Trident and the Rocket-3. Triumph were also taking an active interest in production racing, with works machines at the 500-miler and Production TT. When they discovered the potential of the new threes, this activity branched out into the Daytona 200-mile race and European endurance races, and founded the F750 category.

Honda were not far behind them, their overhead cam 750-four offering virtually Grand Prix design in roadster trim. They too took an interest in the prestige Daytona race and produced performance kits to uprate the 750's power.

In France the motorcycling climate was judged healthy enough for the Bol d'Or to be reinstated, at Montlhéry, although it was soon moved to the more suitable Bugatti circuit at Le Mans. With Gallic shrewdness, the new event had pretty vague rules. At first it catered

Taking over where Godier-Genoud left off, the Pipart Kawasaki is typical of Continental endurance racers
(photo by John Robinson)

simply for two types of machine, those under 250 cc and those above this capacity. As bikes like the 500 Suzuki and Kawasaki were added to the existing European models, they incorporated a 500 and an over-500 class but soon this was abandoned in favour of an open event, up to 1000 cc. And later still, when people started producing 1-litre machines, they lifted the capacity limit to 1200 cc.

Meanwhile in 1969 the new Bol d'Or, although a 24-hour event and eminently suited to an endurance series, was judged not to have enough regulations to be included in the FIM's new *Coupe d'Endurance*. When the Bol d'Or made its rules even more lax, it didn't seem to do any harm — in fact, as far as the race promoters were concerned, it appeared to be a licence to print money; it was eventually the FIM who changed and brought the race into the endurance series.

The Barcelona race (which had always included a class for prototypes) was won in '69 by Canellas/Rocamera on a factory 360 Bultaco, with a Triumph in second place and a 250 Ossa third. The distinction between prototype and production class was that the latter was based on a homologation rule that 200 models should have been sold. The same year, in the production class, the FIM banned anything with double overhead cams or rotary disc valves, no matter how many had been sold.

In 1970 there was a further development which would help endurance racing. Formula 750 was conceived. Basically it was for production machines but, by listing items as factory-approved optional extras, it enabled Triumph, for example, to fit Fontana forks and brakes, Quaife five-speed gearboxes, Seeley or Rob North frames and generally turn the Trident into a very rapid racer. Although many of the bits used in the works Triumphs were less than easy to obtain, it did encourage development along the lines of the endurance prototypes. A cynic might have judged that the formula was tailor-made for the factory Triumphs (Mike Nedham, who worked at Triumph's experimental shop at Umberslade Hall helped to draft the original formula) but there is no doubt that it worked, at the time. It injected a much needed boost to big bike racing, put four-strokes back on the circuits and effected some parity between European and American road racing.

The rules allowed modifications to bring machines up to full race trim, as long as they were based on production engines. This was ensured by homologation regulations which required that a certain number of machines had been sold. Working within this formula, Suzuki developed quite a competitive racer from their GT750. Kawasaki used their H2 in the same way. Apparently nobody thought that a manufacturer would design and build a real racer and then sell enough of them to satisfy the regulations. Until, that is, Yamaha went ahead and did it.

It wasn't against the rules but when the TZ700 appeared, in 1974, there was a short-lived attempt to ban it. If the FIM heard any eerie chuckles at the time, it was probably Alfred Scott.

In 1970 both the Bol d'Or and the 500-miler allowed prototypes to race. Norton's new Commando, ridden by Peter Williams and Charlie Sanby, won the Thruxton race, with Stan Woods and Frank Whiteway second on a 500 Suzuki. Coincidentally, another 500 Suzuki, ridden by Chemarin and Decombeix, won the 500 class at the Bol d'Or. The overall winners were Tom Dickie and Paul Smart on a works 750 Triumph.

A further development had already taken place which was to prove crucial as the prototypes got bigger and more powerful. Dunlop's K81 tyre, produced for the 750 triples, was showing that it had race potential, too. Designed as a rear tyre, there had been no front fitting to 'match' it until the Triumph racers tried using another K81 the wrong way round. The reason for reversing the direction of the tyre is that its construction leaves an

With the Kawasakis reaching the limit of their development, the new generation of roadsters will have to provide the endurance hardware. This near-standard XS1100 was entered in the '78 Bol d'Or
(photo by John Robinson)

The only place a CBX could be raced in Britain? When the Kawasaki ridden by the Germans Horst Lotz and Horst Rudelt blew up in practice for the Brands Hatch 1000 km, they hastily prepared their roadster CBX and raced that instead   *(photo by John Robinson)*

overlapping joint. Fitted correctly to a rear wheel the motive force of the bike pushes the joint together. On the front wheel, braking forces are applied in the opposite direction and could 'peel' the joint apart – hence it was fitted the reverse way round. Malcolm Uphill had used K81s on his 650 Triumph to win a Production TT and become the first production rider to lap the Isle of Man course at more than 100 mph. Because of this the tyres were named TT100. Giving grip and handling which

suited the new bikes, they did not wear out as fast as racing tyres and were used extensively in long-distance races.

The works Triumphs, managed by Doug Hele, were becoming unbeatable. With riders Smart, Jefferies, Tait, Dickie, and Pickrell, they had an ideal blend of racers who were quick but experienced and who had the humour which helps a team to operate efficiently in difficult conditions. The bikes were as quick as anything else on the circuits and more reliable than most. Unfortunately Hele was given neither the support nor the resources to develop the project any further, or to provide any useful feedback for future roadsters.

Triumph helped pave the way for the big racer but other racers were about to take over. Hondas were appearing with big-bore motors and 'Daytona' race kits. Other factories like Ducati and Laverda used the prototype class to develop prototypes and new roadsters.

In '73 a new Ducati 860 V-twin won at Barcelona, the bike later going into production. The same year John Williams and Charlie Williams won the Spa 24-hour race on a semi-official, CB750-based machine, entered by Alf Briggs.

As a result of their racing successes, both Laverda and Ducati offered race kits for their sports models, featuring a replacement fairing and tank, bigger carburetters, camshafts, exhausts and, in the case of the Laverda, a lower frame and a duplex rear chain.

Endurance racing was really taking off, the continental events becoming richer and more prestigious. In Australia a 6-hour production machine race was launched. But the British round still struggled to attract spectators. Several attempts had been made to liven it up, including a move to Brands Hatch. In '75 it was shortened to a 400-mile race and later still, moved back to Brands as 1,000 km race. Unfortunately the British organisers didn't seem to have the flair to put on a meeting with sufficient interest and excitement for the spectators. There was one attempt, at Thruxton, to liven up the proceedings by running a shorter, F750 race,

The Sports Motorcycles Ducati, built for Mike Hailwood, was also ridden at Brands – by George Fogarty and Charlie Sanby *(photo by John Robinson)*

Development

among the endurance racers. The F750s started after the others and had to force their way past the slower bikes. It was probably a lot more exciting for the riders than the spectators, who were more confused than ever.

Even when the machines got more interesting than production bikes and had official works support, the event offered only the race to watch. For many people it was difficult enough to follow that as the sign-posted results were less than comprehensive compared with, say, Le Mans or Spa where the first 12–20 bikes are clearly displayed and the results updated every hour.

The final lack of co-ordination came in '78 when the date of the British round of the Coupe d'Endurance clashed with a Sheene v. Roberts battle at Donington.

By the mid-70s, the racers had taken over endurance racing and in turn had given way to the purpose-built prototypes. While big twins had been the bikes to beat on British circuits, lightweights had been winning on the Continent. These, helped along by the Spanish manufacturers, went their own way, emerging as little more than racers with lights — but with remarkable reliability. These 125, 175, 250 and eventually 360 two-stroke singles could keep up the pace of big four-strokes and last just as long. Quicker roadsters began to get into the results but it wasn't long before the prototypes took over completely.

Chapter Three
The racers take over

In endurance events, pure racing machines grew from being merely tolerated to being a part of the whole show. During certain periods the racers came out on top – the Norton of Lefèvre and Briand was a regular winner at the Bol d'Or, and factory-prepared lightweight prototypes had a lot of good results at Barcelona. But the time and distance involved in the gruelling events was a great equaliser. The endurance factor favoured no one, but it offered a lot of scope for the reliability and regularity of roadster-based machines.

Eventually, when suitable power units became generally available, it was possible to build racer performance into endurance bikes. The racers did take over, but it wasn't pure, short-circuit machines which dominated long-distance races, it was the purpose-built bikes, the ones designed to cope with 24 hours at maximum effort. After this time the genuine roadsters, particularly the smaller ones, had a diminishing chance of getting into the prize money.

In some ways it was the prize money which

One of the Rob North-framed Tridents at scrutineering
(photo by Motorcycle Mechanics)

'Real' racers have often figured in endurance events. Pat Evans shared the Sonauto TZ700 with Boinet at the '76 Bol d'Or. Although fast enough to take the lead it was too thirsty and too fragile to hold it
(photo by Motorcycle Mechanics)

stimulated the development of endurance bikes — not only the money but also the prestige and even the sheer satisfaction of completing one of motorcycling's toughest tests. As the events grew more popular, the rewards grew with them and, in the atmosphere surrounding these events, so did the status of those taking part. This amounted to a powerful incentive — the financial rewards were only a part, but they weren't to be disregarded. In the mid-70s, the winner at the Bol d'Or could look forward to a prize of 50,000F with perhaps a further 30,000F in contingency money. So there was the equivalent of £10,000 floating around for those who tried hard enough. To keep that in perspective: it amounted to nearly three years' pay for an average UK citizen.

Development, in any field, is a series of leap-frog steps and jumps. An improvement in one area, for instance a more powerful engine, demands other improvements, such as chassis and tyres. Luck, or

chance, plays a part in this too; given one improvement, other aspects will eventually catch up and the whole thing will reach a certain level and stay there. Until, that is, someone who happens to be in the right place at the right time comes up with a new idea and the whole sequence begins again.

Before the four-cylinder Japanese engines arrived, endurance racing had reached this kind of stagnation. Most development was left to privateers and was confined to details. There was works support from BMW and Triumph but this was restricted to showing off standard machines — or what purported to be standard machines.

In the case of the Triumph Tridents, the factory could, by using 'optional extras' build machines which were substantially faster than the stock item. Doug Hele and his development team deserve credit for these achievements and it is unfortunate that they couldn't put any of it back into roadster development.

The John Player Nortons, put together, not to say held together, by Peter Williams, came close to being roadsters converted into long-distance racers. They were continually up against the problems of the power unit and although they were raced in a variety of events from F750 through to the TT races, it is ironic that they never performed well in endurance.

Some of the most incredible performances were by

lightweights. The French Ydral machines were regular competitors at the Bol d'Or where these small racers were able to keep up the pace alongside much bigger machines. The others were the Spanish two-strokes and the Italian Ducati singles. The 24-hour race at Barcelona catered for prototypes right from from the mid-50s and although the factories were racing on home territory and under rules which they had helped formulate, this doesn't detract from their performance. To build 125, 175 and 250 machines to road-race specifications and make them last for 24-hours at a go, is a genuine achievement.

The sort of bikes they were up against were, typically, the BMW twins. These machines were famous for the way they combined handling with ride comfort and this in itself made the bikes more than equal to machines with superior performance. In many ways the flat twins were ideal for endurance racing and the German factory took advantage of this with works entries and works support for privately-entered machines.

Ergonomics is one thing ... this Moto Guzzi also had automatic transmission

(photo by Motorcycle Mechanics)

The racers take over

Nevertheless the single-cylinder two-strokes campaigned by Montesa, Ossa and Bultaco were capable of beating them. As the level of racing progressed, the Spanish factories had to build bigger machines, winding up with 360 cc singles. No one has found a way of building a bigger two-stroke cylinder which works and, faced with the need for multi-cylinder design and liquid cooling in order to stay in the game, the Spanish factories had to back out. Fortunately for them, their designs were highly adaptable and the knowledge they had gained allowed them to diversify into off-road sports with no little success.

It was the latest generation of road bikes which caused the trouble. Along with the Trident came the four-cylinder 750 from Honda, the three-cylinder two-stroke from Kawasaki, and Suzuki's two-stroke twin. These machines elevated roadster performance – putting it into the racing class – without losing the reliability of

The Gus Kuhn BMW had extra braces on the frame and swing-arm. The front tyre is a TT100, matched with a semi-slick rear tyre

(photo by Motorcycle Mechanics)

machines which could be used as ride-to-work mounts.

These bikes were to be the innovation which then demanded further development. Their engines were fantastic, combining untold levels of performance with reliability. But they were heavy and didn't handle at all well. At the time it was easier to develop the engines; with conventional tuning it was possible to make the machines so fast in a straight line that handling was of secondary importance – given good enough riders, they could win.

Honda had racing kits developed from their Daytona machines; Kawasaki produced the H1R version of their H1B road bike. Both of these machines were used in long-distance events, although some teams felt that the H1B was fast enough not to need the extra fragility and handling problems of the H1R.

Motorcycle Mechanics magazine ran a 500 Suzuki and then a 500 Kawasaki in long-distance races. The machines were on loan from the importers – initially from

Agrati, who handled Kawasaki, and later from Kawasaki UK, when the franchise was handed to the wholly-owned subsidiary.

An H1R engine had been offered but was turned down because similar machines used by continental teams had proved unreliable. The original 500 was superseded by an H1E and this model, with a standard engine and only chassis modifications, was fast enough to win the 500 class in the Production TT and set a lap record. Yet in the continental endurance events it was totally outpaced by the new breed of bikes. Other developments had allowed the new engines to be used to the full – there were new tyres, for a start. The H1E could just about last a 24-hour race on a pair of K81 Dunlops –

One of the mainstays of endurance events – the race-kitted three-cylinder Laverda

(photo by Rod Sloane)

the bigger, heavier and more powerful bikes needed more, and they were about to get it.

The racing tyres available up to this point gave good grip – on light racers – but on the big endurance bikes they wore too quickly and couldn't cope with the tendency of the heavy bikes to weave. The K81s provided an interim solution, but better tyres were on the way.

Along with tyres, there was a general need to find better chassis – which is precisely what the Godier-Genoud team did, leading to the situation where the purpose-built specials finally dominated endurance racing.

The design of a new frame and cycle parts coincided with the availability of several new items, all of which were to prove crucial to endurance racing. There were new tyres, disc brakes, cast wheels and better dampers, all available at roughly the same time.

These items, with the new engines, quickened the

pace of endurance racing until it reached the point where quick-fill tanks and quick-release wheels became necessary. By this time the racing was so close that pit stops became crucial. The teams needed the right equipment and good mechanics to keep their machines going and pit drill had to be carefully rehearsed. Regulations varied but typically only two people were allowed to work on the bike at the same time – sometimes the rider could remain seated on the bike to hold it up, as long as he did no work.

The ritual in the pits became nearly as important as the riding of the bike – in a long-distance race it was important to keep moving; each second lost in the pits could not be regained. The team was made up of several people – a team manager, timekeepers, a couple of mechanics and the riders. It was the team manager's job to work out the team's tactics, to be prepared for mechanical failures and to bring the bike in for refuelling and work to be done. From performance in practice, he would work out how far the bike could go before refuelling and when tyre and brake changes were likely to be necessary.

Often the timing of pit stops was crucial – generally it

An OW31 in endurance trim: special chassis, alternator and two-way radio

(photo by John Robinson)

Patrick Pons on the Sonauto Yamaha he shared with Christian Sarron, sweeps around a National Motos Kawasaki. The light weight and performance of the Yamaha kept it in the lead for 17 hours during the '78 Bol d'Or but eventually the crankshaft failed
(photo by John Robinson)

was best to let the bike run as long as it could, bringing it in when there were only a couple of litres left in its tank. Then there was the risk that the tank would run dry. It proved important to keep in touch with the rider, using pit signals to relay his lap times, and of course to let him know when to refuel. It was all too easy for the signaller to miss the bike, or for the rider to miss the signal, especially in the dark, and teams rigged up reflective signal boards. Honda Britain used a countdown system to bring the rider in; three laps before his stint ended, he'd be given a sign reading '3', then '2', and finally '1', to avoid the possibility that the rider might miss just one signal. Other teams used two-way radio, which was banned at first but permitted finally at the '78 Bol d'Or. A headset was installed in the rider's helmet, operated by a button on the handlebar, and a small transmitter was mounted in the seat hump.

The refuelling stops themselves could be quite impressive. The bikes would come in along the pit road, often travelling too quickly as the rider tried to readjust to the new conditions and peered through a fly-spattered visor into the brightly-lit bays to locate his own pit. Most teams would have a man holding a sturdy board, first for

the rider to recognise and second, to run into if he underestimated the final stop.

As the motor cut out a mechanic would slam the quick-fill hose into the side of the tank, watching the overflow carefully to see when the tank was full. The rider would sit back, supporting the bike, and another mechanic would check the oil, topping up if necessary, by using a large syringe. With the bike replenished, a quick wipe over the screen and headlamps, a look at the tyres, and the rider would get off on one side while his partner hopped into place from the other. As the bike was paddled out of the pits, a mechanic pushing to start the engine, the other mechanic would scramble along on all fours, spraying the drive chain with lubricant. The whole thing could take less time than it does to read about it.

The racers take over

The quick-fill equipment consists of a large header tank, mounted high up on a framework and replenished from a supply of five-gallon drums, using a hand pump. A large-bore hose with a special nozzle and a valve connects the dump tank to the motorcycle via a diaphragm valve in the side of the bike's tank. This valve lets fuel in under pressure from the dump tank but closes when the hose is snapped out of place.

Originally, a normal filler cap in the top of the tank would be opened, to let air out and to let the mechanic see when the tank was full. Another flap valve in the top vent was supposed to release air and close when the tank was full. This wasn't altogether satisfactory, partly because the mechanic had to force the hose into place and hold it to prevent spillage and this meant he had trouble seeing into the tank. Then, the fuel went in so fast

that it could spray out through the top filler cap and often it surged, leaving an air pocket in the tank. So there was the danger of fuel being sprayed all over the place and the risk of the bike leaving with its tank considerably less than full. This meant that it could quite easily run dry before the next scheduled stop.

To combat these problems, overflow pipes were used which released the top valve in the tanks. The pit crew would fill the tank until fuel came out of the overflow and spilled out into a second tank, held in place by a mechanic. The big dump tanks were also calibrated so that the team manager could see precisely how much fuel the bike had taken.

For longer pit stops, when tyres or brake pads had to be replaced or other adjustments made, the bike would be wheeled on to a stand. These were often ingenious trolley-like devices – the incoming rider would stop the bike in position, a mechanic would lean back on the stand and hoist the whole machine (and sometimes the rider) clear of the ground. The stand would hold the bike steady, with both wheels off the floor so that work could be done on it.

The pit crew had to be carefully rehearsed for these

The Sonauto OW31 was prepared by Christian Maingret for the 24-hour race. It featured strengthened exhausts and quickly-detachable components. There was no generator, the battery being replaced at each stop during the night *(photo by John Robinson)*

A prototype in the true sense of the word – Laverda's liquid-cooled, shaft-drive V-6. The engine is a stressed part of the frame, the long, triangulated swing-arm pivoting on the gearbox casting

(photo by John Robinson)

jobs as well. The team would know roughly when to expect a long pit stop, for example when tyres had to be changed, and would arrange for other jobs to be done at the same time. The mechanics then had to know precisely which jobs to do and the sequence to do them in – partly so that they didn't get in one another's way and partly so that they didn't break the rule about too many people touching the bike at the same time. As one job was completed and the mechanic moved clear, another would move in to do his job or hand new parts, like brake pads, to his partner.

To be able to work as efficiently as possible the pit crew needed the right equipment, often rigging up small generators at the back of the pits to use floodlights around the bike and even power tools. The array of equipment, from ordinary hand tools through to welding equipment, plus spares, was impressive. On most machines it is easier to change many parts as complete assemblies, and the racers had several systems, such as electrical equipment, specifically built this way. To solve a carburation fault, for example, it would be quicker to change the whole bank of carburetters, rather than fiddle around with an individual unit on the bike. So all these spares had to

be stocked in the pits; often a complete machine would be kept, as the most convenient way of storing every individual item, plus routine parts like spark plugs, brake pads and wheels.

With the need to keep all this in check, the team manager's experience of previous races was invaluable. He had to predict the future as well as control the present. Not surprisingly, the better organised and carefully-rehearsed teams could save a lot of time in their pit stops and the closer the competition out on the track, the more important the pit stop became.

As the racing got this close it became necessary to find other ways of going faster and the next step was to look for more horsepower. This would need better reliability and still more efficient pit maintenance and so the cycle began again.

The racers take over

When performance increased, one of the first casualties was tyres. The K81 Dunlops would see a machine like the 500 Kawasaki through a complete 24-hour race, but the one-litre four-strokes, dealing out nearly twice as much power and weighing half as much again, were a different matter.

Dunlop's K70 roadster tyre had taken over from the old 'Universal' type and in the works-supported Grand Prix battles of the '60s, Dunlop had produced their racing KR73 and KR76 tyres. These were the famous 'triangular' tyres, designed to put more rubber on the road as the bikes were heeled into corners. From experience gained with the growing power of the GP Yamahas and Hondas, Dunlop combined profile, tread pattern and compound to get the ultimate in roadholding from these machines. This knowledge eventually found its way back into roadster tyres at the end of the '60s

The six-cylinder engine is no wider than an air-cooled four and gives more ground clearance. Fuel injection was planned but Dell'Orto carburetters were fitted
(photo by Rod Sloane)

when Dunlop produced the K81. This semi-triangular tyre was a spin-off from the KR73. Advances in compound technology — dealing with the blend of natural and synthetic rubbers which makes up the tyre — had produced a material which combined good grip with an acceptable wear rate. The tread pattern was based on the way racing tyres had worn, on the grounds that the scuffing shown on these tyres represented the stresses suffered by the tyre in use. Dunlop had also experimented with small cuts or 'sipes' in the tyre in order to assist the main tread in draining water from under the tyre. The result was tyres which gave remarkably good all-weather adhesion.

When the first big racers appeared, these tyres were an obvious choice. The alternative racing tyres gave more grip but they wore at a proportionally higher rate and their profiles didn't match the heavy machines' requirements.

After Uphill's Bonneville became the first production machine to lap the TT course at over 100 mph — using the new tyres — they were quickly renamed TT100 and went on to become the most extensively used tyres, all over the world.

The bigger machines, like the Kawasaki Z1, took

Alternator mounted above the gearbox on the Dholda RCB. The transparent float bowls are standard fitting on all the RCB engines

(photo by John Robinson)

these excellent tyres to their limits. And when the time came to extract more power still from the big engines, the tyres just couldn't cope. But by this time Dunlop had taken an active interest in endurance racing, developing a new racing tyre, the KR91, specifically for the big bikes. This was a patterned rear tyre with a round profile to suit the heavier bikes and coming in 4.25/85 or 4.70/85 sizes. The /85 means an 85 per cent aspect ratio: that is, the height of the tyre section measures 85 per cent of its width. This was the first time that a tyre had been developed purely for endurance racing, and it was probably used with a KR84 racing tyre, or the good old K81, on the front.

Once again, roadsters were soon to benefit from racing developments. The K91 Red Arrow was produced as a direct result of the KR91 and Dunlop's experience in the construction of slick racing tyres.

The performance of the endurance racers got to the point where they could benefit from slicks, as well, largely because the more rigid structure of the unpatterned tyres allowed the use of 'softer' compounds. These 'soft' or 'sticky' compounds gave formidable grip. By 1976 they were beginning to play with slicks and hand-cut pat-

terned tyres – endurance racers were converging with the bigger GP machines in this respect. Dunlop were using their GP moulds to produce tyres of different construction for the endurance bikes but, of course, where endurance racers were concerned, tyre life was as important as grip and it was well-known that you could have either one or the other but not both. Then, in '78, Dunlop came up with the highly unlikely prospect of a compound which *would* give both...

By 1977 the RCB Hondas were using 5.75 and 6 inch slicks but although these tyres were giving amazing performances, they didn't solve all the problems facing the endurance teams. In many of the longer races, particularly at Spa and Le Mans, the weather could be expected to change considerably during the race. Obviously slicks couldn't be used on wet roads but intermediate or wet weather tyres could only be used at a reduced pace if the road dried out. The reason is that the patterned tyres are more flexible than the slicks and, in the same conditions, tend to run hotter. At very high speeds the tyres can overheat and the tread can break up. The choice of tyres and the decisions to bring a bike in to change to another type often proved critical.

The conditions on the 8.8-mile road circuit at Spa made matters even worse. Set in the hilly Ardennes forest, the track is long enough for the weather conditions to vary from one part to another. The area virtually generates its own weather, as well. Bright sunshine brings mist steaming out of the pine forest, clouds rapidly build ul and sudden, torrential downpours are not at all unusual. In addition to that, the circuit is abnormally fast, allowing the bikes to reach phenomenally high speeds – 180 mph has been quoted – along the long, Masta straight. The RCB of Léon/Chemarin lapped the circuit at an average of more than 126 mph and maintained an overall average speed of just over 115 mph, to cover a distance of 2,771 miles in 24 hours.

'Real' racers have cropped up in endurance racing for many years, some, like the Manx Norton, with more success than others. But none have done well at the Belgian round of the endurance series. In fact Honda-powered machines have won every race since '72 and in 1971 it was the Brown/Rollason 500 BSA which took the overall victory. Always in the running, often with second or third places, came the Belgian father and son team of Jules and Charly Nies riding first a BMW and later a Japauto.

There were earlier 24-hour events in Belgium, at Warsage. The 1971 and 1972 races were held at Zolder and afterwards the Spa-Francorchamps National road circuit was used.

So on the long, hard Belgian National circuit it has always been the roadster-based machines or the purpose-built endurance bikes which have done well. Other circuits had completely different characteristics – the small two-strokes had no trouble on the tightly winding roads at Montjuich Park, despite the length of the race and the high daytime temperatures, which can hardly have favoured this type of machine.

The shorter races offer more chance of a free-for-all but the endurance specialists usually manage to stay ahead of the pure racers. In 1974, the year Godier and Genoud switched to Kawasaki, winning the Barcelona race and the Bol d'Or, and coming second at Spa, it was a totally different Kawasaki which won the Thruxton 500-

The tall frame identifies this as a 76 RCB. Honda used CV carburetters to get easier starting and more flexibility, even though slide carburetters of a similar size could give more power

(photo by Motorcycle Mechanics)

miler. This was the 750 cc H2R two-stroke triple — the original green meanie — ridden by Ballington and Ditchburn. Ironically this was also the year when the FIM tried to ban the TZ700 Yamaha from F750 racing and the first year in which one appeared at the Bol d'Or.

By this time the endurance specialists had really taken over and it was a highly specialised business, with no shortage of competition. In '75 the works Ducati ridden by Grau/Canellas won at Barcelona, the Ruiz/Huguet Japauto won at Spa, Godier/Genoud on the SIDEMM Kawasaki won the Bol d'Or and a similar machine ridden by Luc/Vial won at Thruxton. Just as endurance racing was getting into top gear at other events, the Thruxton race was shortened to 400 miles.

It is this variety, of the circuits, of the race distances, and of the machinery, which gives endurance racing a charm of its own. The teams are working and racing in an atmosphere of complete freedom — freedom to race any machine they choose, and freedom to prepare it any way they choose — and their innovations can only add to the attraction.

Since 1976, design philosophy, if not individual design, has crystallised but there is still much room for development, unless 'The Formula' is applied to this class of racing. A look at a typical endurance racer will show the current state of the art and the areas where new technology and developments might improve things.

The engine needs to be capable of perhaps 130 bhp or at least enough to propel the machine to speeds in excess of 160 mph. It also has to be easy to start and reasonably flexible, with usable power spread over a band of 3,000 rpm. The 1000 cc engines probably represent an acceptable limit — 1200 cc is permissible but already the engines are too wide, too tall and too heavy. They are tuned to the point where they become violent, and they need to be painstakingly prepared for maximum reliability.

One problem is to make the engine breathe efficiently at high speeds and large carburetters are used, usually 32 or 34 mm on a four-cylinder engine compared with around 28 mm on a similar roadster. They will also use bigger valves but the cams will not be too violent, to avoid making the engine 'peaky' and the machine hard to ride. One problem with bigger valves and higher valve lift is that it makes piston design more complicated and, of course, the pistons need to give as high a compression ratio as possible. A piston with a high dome has to have sufficient crown thickness to tolerate deep cutaways for the valves, and this results in a heavy piston and greater inertia loading on the connecting rod and big end.

Honda found a way round this problem by using four-valve cylinder heads. The optimum lift for a valve is proportional to its diameter — even if the cam lifts the valve further the port will not flow more gas. So two smaller valves, instead of one big valve, require less lift.

Therefore it is easier to use higher compression ratios without the problem of the valves touching the pistons. The valves themselves are smaller and considerably lighter and the cam doesn't have to move them so far, so the inertia loadings are much reduced which means that the valve gear will tolerate higher engine speeds.

Without the facility to make this kind of modification or to make the engine withstand higher inertia loadings, the Kawasaki fours had reached the end of their development.

To seek out more power would mean either raising the engine speed or raising the bmep — the pressure level — of the engine. To go to a larger engine would create as many problems as it would solve, in size and weight.

Raising the engine speed also increases the inertia loading and the problems of friction at the moving parts. But there is a bigger obstacle — making the engine breathe at higher speed. Volumetric efficiency drops off as the speed gets higher, simply because there is less time for the gas to get into the cylinder. Holding the valves open longer would help, but only at the expense of making the power band narrower. For the gain to be significant, it would entail an unacceptable loss in flexibility. So the only way to make use of higher engine speed is to find something more efficient than the four-valve head — which is a future possibility.

Raising the bmep is another way of getting more power at the same speed; again it involves getting more gas into the engine or raising the compression, both of which present practical problems. Even if it were achieved, the increased heat level would probably demand liquid-cooling.

Racers currently use exhaust designs which enhance the power — the FIM noise limit is quite generous compared to the restrictions imposed on roadsters — and the optimum exhaust system can add as much as 25 per cent to the power output of a stock roadster engine.

New technology may provide an answer in materials which can withstand increased thermal stress, and may, for example, permit rotary valve designs to become practical. An alternative course lies in the power still wasted in the exhaust, if this can be fed back into the engine as useful energy. A turbocharger performs this task and, although one hasn't yet been tried in endurance racing, it is about the only class of motorcycle racing where such a development might be acceptable.

As long as the engine could stand the higher, overall level of power — again it would probably require liquid-cooling — the turbocharger offers a couple of clear advantages. A turbocharger can double the output of a naturally-aspirated engine, which means that a smaller engine could be used to start with. Then, because it is working from energy which would normally be wasted, there is the benefit of more efficient running either as increased power or as a more economical unit — and fuel

Waiting for the rain – the Honda Britain pit at Spa during practice for the 1977 race. From the left on the pit counter, rider Stan Woods, Tony Rutter and team manager Alf Briggs look thoughtful as Roger Marshall gets ready for his first ride

(photo by Motorcycle Mechanics)

consumption is important in long-distance races. A charged engine can also be more reliable than one which depends upon atmospheric pressure. The reason is that to get high outputs without a blower involves high compression which, in turn, causes a very high pressure when the mixture is ignited. This pressure reaches a very high peak and then falls rapidly, whereas in a blown engine the peak pressure level can be kept a lot lower, although the *average* pressure during the working stroke is higher. So the piston need not be subjected to sudden, excessive pressures.

There is always a snag and in the case of the turbocharger, it is that no one has made a unit small enough to match motorcycle engines over a reasonable speed range. Furthermore, with any blower there are carburation problems, although fuel injection may be a possible cure for that.

Going back to existing machinery, the race engines already have special connecting rods and probably an increased oil supply, with either a larger reservoir or an oil cooler. They run electronic ignition systems, for reliability at high rpm and for their lack of maintenance, plus the fact that they can run with their own, small generator as a self-contained system. This is convenient because it means the ignition is independent of the lighting system and the ignition generator can be mounted on one of the camshafts.

That is part of the next step – to remove as much as possible from the ends of the crankshaft and so reduce engine width. The alternator is usually relocated above the gearbox, perhaps driven by the original starter motor gear, or from a pulley mounted on the gearbox sprocket. Others have simply mounted the generator on the sprocket, so that it only works when the machine is in motion. One team even rigged up a fan-driven generator, mounted outside the fairing to be powered by the airstream but the scrutineers rejected the idea.

The development of the big machines can be traced back through claimed horsepower figures – bearing in mind that claimed figures for a racer do not always owe allegiance to a dynamometer.

In 1970 the works Trident produced 70 bhp at 8,000 rpm and the bulkier Honda 750 claimed 75–80 bhp. Figures quoted for the following year's Honda – by the people who raced them in France, not necessarily the factory – were down to 70–75 bhp.

Laverda and Moto Guzzi were claiming 68 and 60 bhp respectively, while the 500 BSA single, which was often among the leaders, was alleged to produce 36 bhp at 6,500 rpm. That possibly says something for lack of bulk.

The SIDEMM Kawasakis, in '73, gave 96 bhp at 9,000 rpm, compared with the 750 Suzuki's 95 bhp at 7,000 and the CB750 plus racing kit, which upped the power to 90 bhp.

By 1976 the SIDEMM Kawasakis were up to 102 bhp at the back wheel, which Georges Godier estimated as 110–115 bhp at the crankshaft, tallying with the 115 bhp of the 76 RCB. The 78 RCBs were giving 130 bhp or more which is what the 0W31 Yamahas are supposed to produce.

The paper performance of these machines makes interesting comparisons but it also translated quite successfully into performance on the track. On most circuits the endurance bikes set lap times only marginally slower than the 500 GP racers; in '77 Christian Léon broke Lucchinelli's lap record at the Nürburgring during official practice. Unfortunately he crashed in the race, so the RCB's performance couldn't be seen over any length of time.

The big engines, even after they had been radically trimmed back, still caused problems. Their weight was one and their width was another. The engine had to be mounted high in the frame in order to get ground clearance for cornering. By the time a 24-litre fuel tank was added, the machine could be pretty tall. Most chassis designs kept the engine up high and gave a reasonably low riding position and low frontal area. Some had repositioned fuel tanks – pannier tanks alongside the engine, tanks built in under the rider's seat or even triangular-section tanks below the engine, with the exhausts running above it.

To cope with the weight, power and size of the engine, the frames were heavily triangulated, with particularly stiff swinging-arm assemblies and steering heads. They obviously gave good handling but to get the necessary strength they were unduly heavy. The best examples start at about 160 kg for the whole machine while the worst examples weigh in at over 220 kg. The weight penalty, on a typical machine, would be

The 77 RCB had lower frame rails, going round the carburetters and the bike was the subject of a major weight-saving exercise

(photo by Honda UK)

equivalent to a rider of an OW31 Yamaha, which has a similar power output, carrying a pillion passenger!

The importance of this aspect can be seen in the inordinate lengths Honda went to in order to reduce weight on their RCB. This included making hollow components or drilling parts and adding carbon fibre to the glass fibre seat and fairing in order to reduce material without losing strength.

The cycle parts were designed for rider comfort, the ability to change or repair them quickly and rapid access to the running gear. Thus, footrests and foot pedals may be mounted on a plate which bolts to the frame, presumably so that it can shear off in a crash and be replaced by another unit. Electrical systems were sometimes quite sophisticated, with additional touches like two-way radio. More often they were very basic, with

direct lighting from the generator or a battery used alone, a recharged battery being fitted at each pit stop.

After the domination of the works Hondas the designs became standardised, in that they met the same requirements, and development of roadster-based engines reached a peak. As with other forms of racing, endurance reached a saturation point where development was concerned. It remains the only form of circuit racing which is essentially free from restrictions and, with new generations of roadsters appearing, there is plenty of scope for further developments. But endurance racing has gained too much prestige; it won the FIM's recognition and is facing plans for World Championship status. This may not be a good thing. Apart from adding one, two, or more World Champions to an already long list, the FIM cannot tolerate regulations which bend with the wind. It is this lack of restriction which has allowed endurance racing to grow and has allowed events such as the Bol d'Or to popularise the racing, literally by making it part of a carnival. The application of 'The Formula' could well stifle both the development and the atmosphere.

Hand-cutting slick tyres, the cottage industry of the race paddock

(photo by Rod Sloane)

Chapter Four
Chassis development

Competitions where stamina, on the part of the rider and his machine, is the chief ingredient have contributed more to chassis development than any other type of sport. The most sophisticated designs are to be found in events like motocross, enduro, and endurance racing. The reasons are simple enough: in these events the chassis and suspension can contribute as much to the machine's performance as the power of the engine. In fact, without the attention to chassis and suspension, a motocross rider would find it difficult to use the engine's performance.

In long-distance road racing the frame, brakes, suspension and all the auxiliary cycle parts play an equally important role. Just like a GP racer, the endurance machines need good handling — more than a pure racing bike because the roadster-based, long-distance bikes are much heavier. But in these long

One of the most successful endurance race designs, the Godier-Genoud Kawasaki. However, by 1976 they had reached the limit of engine development and, without factory support, could not beat the RCB Hondas *(photo by Motorcycle Mechanics)*

Chassis development

events, some covering well over **3,000 km**, the chassis can help in many other ways. It can take the strain off the rider by making the machine comfortable and easy to use. It can increase the life of chains by reducing the changes in chain tension. It can speed up pit stops by

Below **Other specialists worked hard at chassis development. This triangulated frame, built by D'Hollander, carried the wheel in two arms which pivoted above and below the gearbox**
Opposite top **Mead and Tomkinson had a similar approach. This is the rear suspension on their 1976 Laverda. The assembly is very rigid, minimises changes in chain tension and gives rapid access to the rear wheel. It is also very heavy**
(photos by Motorcycle Mechanics)
Opposite bottom **Eventually even the arch-exponents of chassis design had to give in to the might of Honda and the orthodox layout of the RCB**
(photo by John Robinson)

offering quickly-detachable components and rapid, easy access to parts which need maintenance, plus quick-fill fuel and oil tanks. It can protect the rider from the continual strain of the airstream — and more important, from the chilling effects of rain. It can even help in the event of a crash, because a good design will protect vulnerable parts, such as hydraulic circuits, and will have control pedals, etc., mounted so that the whole assembly can be changed quickly.

Chassis design can make a difference in all of these aspects, each one adding a slight amount to the machine's overall performance. Even more important, it can reduce the precious time spent when the bike is at a standstill and this can make all the difference to the race results.

In short Grand Prix races many of these factors do not count for much. If a rider merely slides off, the time lost will probably put him out of the running so it doesn't matter whether the crash only scratches the paintwork or whether it demolishes some crucial part. And, in a sense, a good Grand Prix racer is the wrong man to ask about

Chassis development

handling problems. All he wants is more power and if that ties the frame in knots, he will find some way to manage the bike. The behaviour of pure racing machines has to be seen in relation to the skill and bravery of the rider. And, if the rider complained that his machine was uncomfortable, the team manager could tell him, with some justification, that he wasn't trying hard enough.

So GP bikes haven't contributed very much to chassis improvements. Even when they've had the opportunity, circumstances have made it largely unnecessary. When swinging-arm suspension came along it made quite a difference at first, largely by helping to keep the wheels on the track. But smoother circuits were being built which took away the need. The very action of the suspension emphasised any weakness in the frame and so racers always had very stiff suspension, allowing the minimum of wheel movement.

There were one or two circuits where decent suspension was a definite advantage, one being the long, bumpy TT road circuit. When the swinging-arm Norton was introduced its frame was called 'Featherbed' because of its luxurious qualitites. A famous quotation is attributed to Geoff Duke, after winning a TT on one of these models. During an interview after the race he was offered a seat, but declined it, saying that he'd been lying down all morning. But anyone used to a modern roadster would probably find Duke's Norton slightly harsh,

With the light and relatively low-powered machines then being raced, it wasn't necessary to develop suspension any further. When power outputs rose, ending in the 500 works Honda of the late '60s, there was an obvious need to re-think motorcycle chassis. But future events ruled that possibility out. Honda pulled out of GP racing and the FIM dreamt up new regulations for the GP classes which temporarily inhibited engine development.

Opposite top **A later version, Kawasaki-powered, held the wheel in a box-section arm, with a radius arm controlling the suspension linkage. The front suspension still had hub-centre steering but the caliper had been removed from between the two steering-link struts to a position in front of them. This was to avoid problems caused by run-out in the large wheel bearing** *(photo by John Robinson)*
Opposite bottom **The naked truth. The front suspension is a pivoted fork, wide enough for the wheel to move inside it as it goes from lock to lock. The drag links which control the steering, also operate the single damper which is mounted where the steering head normally lives**
Right **Nicknamed 'Nessie', the M & T's hump contains the upswept exhausts while the fuel tank is slung below the engine. The alternator is driven by a toothed belt** *(photos by Motorcycle Mechanics)*

The result was that as roadsters got bigger and more powerful they also became tremendously heavy and had handling which was considerably less than endearing. There was, it seems, not enough experience to enable the factories to build a big machine which functioned properly.

Motocross racers were having problems of a different kind. Eventually they developed long-travel suspension, dampers that didn't fade and frames which didn't break. Many of these ideas were used in roadster models and even in racing machines which were beginning to need suspension to match the more powerful engines. Tyres had made tremendous improvements and the racers needed some means to use this new power of adhesion.

But it was left to the long-distance racers to do something about taming the new generation of big road bikes. When they got into it seriously, similar improvements soon made their way into the production line. This development really began in the late '60s and early '70s, coinciding with the introduction of Dunlop's K81 tyre.

Endurance racers, however, had long seen the advantages of good chassis design. Right back in the 1920s, people were making small but significant alterations. They were, of course, restricted by 'production' type regulations up until the days of the prototypes. But

Opposite **Eric Offenstadt designed this trailing link fork for his 350 Yamaha. The link carrying the wheel operates two struts to compress a single de Carbon damper carried in front of the steering head**
Below **The Offenstadt chassis had a cast backbone and cantilever rear suspension**
(photos by Motorcycle Mechanics)

there was no rule against adding extra padding to the seat and, as machine modifications became more acceptable, the changes became more radical.

Early development consisted largely of using optimum-sized fuel and oil tanks, for example. Obviously, the larger the tank the longer the bike could run without topping-up; the limit being the extra size and weight needed. Many machines also had a simple sheet of foam rubber folded and strapped across the seat and tank to give the rider a more cushioned journey.

Reducing rider fatigue was of major importance in the days when only one rider was permitted. Even the

Below **A later version had the same principles but had been tidied up considerably**
Opposite **The front wheel is now carried in two separate links instead of one loop, and the damper is operated via bell-cranks which pivot on the lower fork yoke** *(photos by John Robinson)*

'strictly standard' bikes had riding positions altered and modified controls. Handlebar levers were often made longer, giving greater leverage and therefore demanding less effort from the rider. One or two sidecar outfits had hydraulically-operated brakes, which offered the benefit that all the brakes could be operated by one foot-pedal. With repositioned footrests, remote gear linkages were necessary and many machines used a rocking-pedal. This took the form of two levers, one pointing forward of the pivot and one pointing back, both joined together, so the rider had only to stamp down, depending on which pedal he chose, to change up or to change down.

Novelties like automatic advance and retard mechanisms for the ignition, and automatic lubrication, doubtless caused great joy among the overworked riders. (Most machines in the '20s and '30s had manual ignition control with cable operation and the rider had to adjust the ignition timing to suit the engine speed. Some machines also had a hand-operated oil pump and if the rider forgot to pump often enough, the engine quickly

reminded him by seizing up.)

Fuel tanks were made about as large as the machine would stand, although outlandish sizes weren't essential as the machine's fuel consumption wasn't as heavy as current racers. Oil tanks were often around the 6-litre mark, the reservoir acting as an oil cooler as well as reducing the times replenishment would be needed.

Oddly enough, fairings did not appear in great numbers. Even in the early '50s, when racing machines were generally accepted, only a few appeared with fairings. The Manx Nortons had their standard fly-screens and the 250 works Puch had a top-half fairing plus a faired front mudguard which doubled up as a number plate. These 250s, which did remarkably well at the Bol d'Or, were very low and sleek, sitting on 16-inch-diameter wheels (compared with earlier racers whose wheels were invariably greater than 20 inches). The 175 Ydral also wore a top-half fairing, a bulbous device which covered the rider's hands. These machines had a 'kneeler' riding position like the experimental Norton of the same era.

Opposite top **The frame of the Gold Wing followed normal practice with its widely-triangulated steering head and the linkage operating the single damper**
(photo by Motorcycle Mechanics)

Opposite bottom **Big, smooth and powerful, the flat-four Gold Wing engine had a lot of promise – on paper – and made a neat installation for this racer built by Honda Suisse. The diaphragm valve for the quick filler shows that the fuel tank extends from above the swing-arm pivot to its normal position and the same structure also carries the battery**
(photo by Motorcycle Mechanics)

Below **Japauto, a Parisian Honda dealer, have concentrated on big-bore engines, cycle parts and race back-up rather than chassis design. With several endurance victories to their credit, they produced this variant for '76. This one was powered by a CB750-based motor while a similar model had a borrowed RCB engine**

(photo by Motorcycle Mechanics)

9

40ème BOL D'OR

revêtement réfléchissant
Scotchlite 3M

The fairings grew and by the mid-50s the Ydral and the Gnôme et Rhône 175s had full, dustbin fairings, completely enclosing the front wheel. The FIM ban on total enclosures put a stop to any further development along these lines.

Apart from the Spanish works prototypes, other specials were appearing by the end of the '50s. The winner of the 250 class at the 1957 Bol d'Or had an Adler engine in an AGF frame. And by the end of the '60s there were plenty of hybrid machines, like the Triumph/Norton specials prepared by Dresda, or specials using the Rickman Metisse frame.

The original Japauto special was based on the 750 Honda, its 61 x 63 mm engine being taken out to 70 x 63 mm, using pistons from the CB450 twin. This, running on standard carburetters and modified, 4-pipe exhausts, was fitted into a stock frame. It also had a huge, humped seat, a 25-litre Read Titan fuel tank and a three-piece Churchgate fairing which carried two additional spotlamps. The whole thing weighed 215 kg.

A short while later, the Egli-framed Honda used by Godier and Genoud showed a more positive approach. At only 170 kg, it featured items like cast wheels and a four-into-one exhaust. Its 8-litre oil tank lasted a full 24-hour race without topping up and also did away with the need for an oil cooler. By this time, though, Japauto had a Dresda frame and, at Le Mans, they beat the Godier machine, the two bikes finishing first and second.

The bigger, heavier and more powerful machines demanded careful consideration. No other engines were quite as suitable, yet this posed its own problems. The chassis not only had to meet the racer's requirements of minimum size and weight with maximum strength, it also had to provide typically roadster needs for lighting, comfort and weather protection.

With riders under less stress than in a GP, and spreading their concentration over a full 24 hours, comfort took on a lot of importance. Comfort in this sense really means ergonomics rather than luxury. Because

Opposite **The RCB-powered version used only one rear damper. Its box-section swing-arm was braced by a secondary loop, giving ample stiffness. With the machine on its stand, the amount of suspension movement can be seen**
Below **For '77 the Japauto had begun to look slightly more conventional** *(photos by Motorcycle Mechanics)*

long-distance racing was not as prestigious as the GPs, most of the riders weren't up to the standards of their GP counterparts and this made attention to the handling, and so on, of the machines even more important. You couldn't ask a rider to make up for deficiencies in the machine, and keep it up for such long periods of time. In these circumstances, making the bike easier to ride was as important as finding more power.

There were basically three different attempts at a solution to this problem. The first group opted for, or were stuck with, less powerful units. The second group tried to use racers, adding the bare minimum of auxiliary equipment. The third group tried to tame the big bikes.

The first group were the most successful initially, although the lightweight, factory racers often came out on top. Works-prepared machines from Triumph, BMW, Ducati and so on had sufficient power without the penalty of real bulk. With conventional modifications they worked quite well — ironically, stiffer suspension was usually one of these modifications. The later Tridents, based on the Daytona machines, used a Rob North frame.

Peter Williams, stuck with the over-developed Norton twin, *had* to develop a chassis to compensate for the lack of engine. While he was running a small race team from the Andover competition shop, many original ideas flowed from his fertile mind. The Nortons appeared with monocoque chassis, rigidly triangulated lightweight frames, cantilever suspension, cast wheels, pannier fuel tanks and aerodynamically developed fairing and seat units. Any of these designs could have laid the foundation for future development and for roadster design. But the engine could barely match its contemporaries for power, much less for reliability.

Opposite top **The '78 machine kept basically the same layout, with detail changes to the frame and cycle parts**
Opposite bottom **There have been more variants on the big Kawasaki than any other machine. The Pipart Kawasaki uses cantilever rear suspension with a single de Carbon damper. This model, entered at the '78 Bol d'Or, was also equipped with two-way radio**
Below **This frontal shot of two of the Pipart Kawasakis emphasises the need to reduce frontal area and the problems with width and ground clearance on the in-line fours**

(photos by John Robinson)

Chassis development

On a smaller scale, other people, like Eric Offenstadt, tried to use lesser engines with monocoque chassis and experimental suspension, in a bid to make handling and rideability equal to horsepower. The attempts weren't without success but they were a year or two too late.

Peter Williams tried many variations on the Nortons, including cast swing-arms, cantilever suspension, aerodynamic fairing design and monocoque chassis *(photo by Motorcycle Mechanics)*

Immediately before the big bikes took over, smaller roadster-based models were doing well. The 500 Suzuki twins, the powerful but evil-handling Kawasaki 500 triples and the 500 BSA single all rang up a steady list of successes in their classes and, quite frequently, in the overall placings.

The reasoning of the people in the second group was simple enough. Any of the current road racers would beat the endurance bikes, so all that was needed was some work to make them last the distance and to fit necessary extras like lighting. Given enough other machines on the

track, well-lit corners, or a brave enough rider, these accessories could be pretty rudimentary.

Spanish lightweight racers had done well enough, particularly at Barcelona, until the late '60s and after that there was a small but regular entry of modified racing Yamahas. First they were the air-cooled TD2 types, with cylinder barrels from roadster Yamaha twins to 'detune' them into reliability. The first real achievement was by a TZ350 in '73, which finished 11th at the Bol d'Or. The following year a TZ700 came 6th, with Offenstadt's 350 Yamaha-powered special right behind it. Things may have looked encouraging for the racer-brigade, but apart from the works H2R Kawasaki winning the Thruxton 500-miler, they haven't bettered this achievement.

This model had pannier fuel tanks to keep the machine and its weight as low as possible. At one stage they used a fuel pump operated by the action of the swing-arm to pump fuel up into a header tank which supplied the carburetters

(photo by Motorcycle Mechanics)

Above **This Moto Guzzi relied on a near-stock chassis. It even retained the linked braking system – the front disc nearest the camera is operated via the foot pedal. The other front disc is connected to the front brake lever**
Opposite top **The works Hondas originally used de Carbon dampers and Lockheed brakes which allowed the pads to be changed quickly**
Opposite bottom **The long-life chain developed by Honda and the riveted Comstar wheels soon found their way onto production machines**
(photos by Motorcycle Mechanics)

A TZ Yamaha set the fastest lap times at the '76 Bol d'Or but it didn't last until half distance. In '78 another specially prepared Yamaha, an OW31 ridden by Pons and Sarron, stayed in the lead for nearly 18 hours but finally retired. At the Brands Hatch 1,000 km race, several Yamahas were entered but didn't get among the leading Hondas.

The third group set about modifying the big, four-cylinder bikes. The weight and power of these machines were becoming too great for the K81 tyre. The rounder-profile tyres made by Michelin and Continental were better suited to these machines. Fortunately, though, endurance racing had become big enough business to attract the interest of the tyre companies and this stimulated competition between Dunlop and Michelin, in particular. The result was better tyres for the competitors – and for roadsters. Dunlop eventually produced their KR91 specifically for endurance racing and from this tyre they developed the roadster K91 – the Red Arrow. Michelin were using their S41 and M45 tyres with varying compounds to suit the track conditions. Again, these were available for roadsters, as was the later M48, developed for the one-litre machines from Michelin's original PV, wet-weather racing tyre. Continental also developed a round profile type, the K111 and K112, specifically for the larger road machines.

From the early '70s new damper units were available – the adjustable Koni and de Carbon types being the most commonly used. Disc brakes were used, with Lockheed or Brembo calipers, as these allowed the pads to be changed quickly. The machines were also fitted with larger fairings, often with additional lights, such as Cibié, built in. Quick-fill fuel tanks were appearing on some of the machines.

Chassis development

The next round of developments centred on these cycle parts. Fairing and seat design became ostentatious, although there was some practicality to it because it provided useful spaces in which to hang oil coolers, batteries, electrical fittings and even reserve fuel tanks or emergency tools. Japauto's 1974 machine had a fairing which might have been styled on a veteran car and inside were extra long brake and clutch levers, to give lighter operation. The brake hydraulics led to twin discs, each with two calipers! It meant that disc runout and align-

Support from the tyre companies proved crucial to the endurance racers. Here David Lamb of Dunlop checks the temperature of an RCB's tyre after Charlie Williams' practice session *(photo by John Robinson)*

ment of the floating calipers became critical but they claimed a more gentle operation and presumably it reduced the need to change pads as often.

While prototype versions of the Guzzi 850, Ducati V twin, BMW 900 and later 980 versions — with extra bracing on the frames — appeared, the special builders managed to stay approximately one jump ahead.

Godier and Genoud finally realised much of the potential in chassis development. The essence of their design was that it made the whole machine an integral unit, catering for all the demands of endurance racing. By 1976 the Godier Kawasakis had run out of engine development but their machines weighed only 167 kg compared with more than 200 kg for the more powerful RCB Honda.

The original Godier-Genoud Kawasakis had 200 mm

of wheel movement and the rear wheel could be replaced in 50 seconds. The frame, designed at IUT Amiens, had a high strength/weight ratio which is necessary for good handling and gave rapid access to all of the parts likely to need maintenance. Integrated electrical circuits allowed quick replacement in the event of damage or failure.

There was much more scope to adjust the rear de Carbon suspension unit than on a conventional frame. Ceriani front forks were used with JPX rims and discs, and Brembo brakes. Taken to the 1000 cc limit, the engine ran 31 mm Keihin carburetters and a four-into-one Devil exhaust. The first version weighed 200 kg, wet.

The problems with the one-litre, four-cylinder engines were also their main attraction. They could produce over 100 bhp in a relatively low state of tune but the engines were wide, tall and heavy. The frame design had to be strong enough to contain the weight and the power without bending in the middle. The width of the engines could be reduced by removing the alternator and anything else that hung on the ends of the crankshaft. In some races, it would be enough to run with only a battery and a total loss electrical system. Otherwise the alternator had to be relocated, usually above the gearbox or on the gearbox sprocket.

Detail design can make a lot of difference; the electrical components are all mounted on one QD board while the alternator is driven from the gearbox to reduce engine width. The footrest and gearshift pedal are also mounted on a single plate
(photo by John Robinson)

Even then the engine width meant that the power unit had to be mounted high up in order to get enough ground clearance for cornering. Most roadsters ground at an angle of 40–45 degrees from the vertical; a racer needs clearance of 50 to 55 degrees.

Apart from the possible penalties of raising the engine mass, it would, in a conventional frame, make the whole machine higher and increase its frontal area. Frontal area is what air resistance resists against and therefore can be equated directly to horse-power. The answer, for most of the special builders, was to construct a frame which went around the engine. They turned the necessary width of the frame into a virtue because it gave a widely triangulated assembly at the steering head as well as providing something to attach the fairing to. On many of the machines the fairing would bolt straight on to the frame and still be wider than the rider's knees. The seat and tank unit would be shaped so that the rider was wedged, as comfortably as possible, somewhere down low in the middle of the bike.

Most machines have stayed with conventional front forks; it was at the back of the bike that the problems showed up. In order to get a swinging-arm assembly that was stiff enough, they either used box-section tubing or triangulated the arm itself. Once this had enough rigidity, it didn't need two spring/damper units – the spring was able to revert to its proper job of suspending the machine and didn't have to brace the swing arm. The need for only one damper proved beneficial – at that time the best dampers which were readily available were those used on F1 racing cars. Such a unit had enough energy-absorption capacity to deal with a bouncing motorcycle on its own. Using only one damper presented a couple of immediate advantages – it saved weight and allowed better access around the rear of the bike. The machines with triangulated swinging arms also had a convenient

Opposite **Frame design has to be complemented by equal attention to the cycle parts. The elaborate lines of this Kawasaki give the rider maximum protection and comfort. Note the width of the frame**
(photo by Motorcycle Mechanics)
Below **The same machine, seen from the side, shows how the twin headlamps are mounted in the fairing and the quick-release fasteners which hold the fairing, tank and seat in place**
(photo by Motorcycle Mechanics)

structure with which to operate the damper.

The Godier-Genoud design had the triangulation running below the line of the conventional swinging arm. From this another linkage operated a bell-crank which compressed the spring unit. The system was not unlike that used by Moto Guzzi many years before, except that the spring sat vertically behind the engine and not horizontally beneath it. This type of suspension gave a lot of scope for adjustment. The damper unit had internal adjustment to control its damping; the spring could be changed to alter the spring rate and the pre-load, or fitted length, of the spring could be adjusted. On top of that, the relative lengths of the linkage could be used to change the machine's ride-height and to control the wheel rate.

One thing that suspension did not do was to prevent the chain tension altering as the wheel moved up and down. The pivot for the suspension was behind the gearbox sprocket so the chain would be at its tightest when the centres of the two sprockets were in line with the pivot. As the suspension moved in bump or rebound, the chain could slacken. The only compensation for this was a small slipper tensioner bearing on the top run of the chain.

Drive chains were becoming more of a problem,

mainly because the powerful bikes wore them out so quickly and the varying tension caused by the suspension only aggravated this problem. Typical suspension movement on a conventional swinging arm alters the length of the chain-line by roughly one per cent. This may not seem excessive but is, in fact, the stretch or wear limit on a racing chain. The considerable load in the chain also interacted with the suspension, causing pitching when power was put on or taken off.

Two solutions were tried. The Belgian Dholda team built a frame in which two pivoted arms carried the rear wheel. The position of the pivots, one above and one

Opposite top **A single seat and tank unit is a common type of design, possibly including a battery carrier in the tail of the seat**
Opposite bottom **Another variation on the same theme, this Kawasaki emphasises the smooth contours of the enclosed, comfortable riding position**
Below **Bringing things down to the basic fundamentals, this machine features single-curvature components making up its fairing and screen**
(photos by John Robinson)

Chassis development

below the gearbox sprocket, and the lengths of the two arms controlled the path followed by the wheel during suspension movement. This could be arranged so that the wheel moved in an arc centred on the gearbox sprocket and therefore kept constant chain tension. The British Mead and Tomkinson team produced a similar frame for their Laverda. This had hub-centre steering as well, so both front and rear suspension were controlled by pivoting radius arms. They later extended this principle, using the relative movement of the rear struts to compress the spring/damper unit. Despite the novelty of the design, the machine was very heavy, weighing 220 kg.

Opposite top **By having the swing-arm pivot on the gearbox, the Laverda prototype is able to eliminate changes in the drive length although this is less beneficial with its shaft-drive layout. Ironically it suffered a drive failure during its first race**
Opposite bottom **Rigidly braced swing-arm assemblies solved many of the handling problems which the big bikes suffered and, incidentally, did away with the need for two damper units**
Below **Moving the fuel down low was obviously the main objective behind this layout**

(photos by John Robinson)

The other solution, used later by Bimota, was to use a single fork, pivoted on the axis of the gearbox sprocket. This ensures constant chain tension but also needs a very wide and very long swinging arm, with a heavily braced frame to support the two bearings. The nature of this frame hampers access to the rear of the engine unit.

When Honda first used the RCB they came up against the same problems — and, of course, already suffered them, to a lesser extent, with their road machines. Their answer was to find a chain which could survive. It wasn't merely a matter of making the links stronger because that would also make them heavier, increasing the chain's tendency to fling off the sprockets at high speed. But they succeeded in developing a 'long-life' chain which worked for the racers as well as the roadsters. Built to precise quality control standards, the chain had pre-greased bearing surfaces and the lubricant was sealed by O-rings. The chains were still sprayed during pit stops to prevent the O-rings drying and deteriorating.

Other styles of rear suspension evolved, each with its own advantages, but none which made life any easier for the chains. Some had a reinforcing loop under the conventional swinging arm, making the assembly stiff enough to need only one damper. This would be mounted in a conventional position but with a choice of mounting points. By altering the angle at which the damper was

installed, there was some control over the effective wheel rate.

Others, like the cantilever Yamaha (and long before that, the Vincent) used the triangulated brace to compress a damper which was anchored to the backbone of the frame.

A refinement on this theme, used in the Dutch Nico Bakker frames, amongst others, was to replace the secondary loop with an adjustable shackle, which bolted to the swinging arm, close to the wheel spindle. The top end of this shackle was attached to a rocker arm which pivoted on the frame. The other end of the rocker operated the spring/damper unit.

Very few attempts have been made to improve on conventional telescopic front forks. Pivoted-link forks can be made stronger than telescopics; also when the suspension compresses, under braking or as the machine goes over a bump, this action can change the castor angle, trail and wheelbase, thus altering the machine's handling properties. Leading link and trailing link forks give the designer more control over these changes and, depending on how the brake torque arm is fitted, can give anti-dive properties under braking. Despite these seemingly desirable qualities, the race teams obviously don't have a problem with telescopic forks.

The Mead and Tomkinson design had the steering pivot located inside the front hub, the wheel being carried on radius arms with a single spring fitted up where the steering head would be on a conventional machine. The problem with this layout is that the wheel bearings need to have a very large diameter — on the early design the disc calipers were carried at the 12 o'clock position on the disc and the machine suffered frequent brake failures. Play in the wheel bearing was causing runout at the disc which was pushing the pads away. When the rider needed to brake he then had to pump the lever to push the pads back to the disc. This was cured by relocating the caliper, moving it to the 9 o'clock position so that it

Opposite top **The heavily triangulated frame of this Martin Kawasaki makes a compact, accessible, yet low structure. With no weight on the rear wheel, it also shows how much variation there can be in chain tension**

Opposite bottom **Classical, Yamaha-type cantilever suspension is a feature of the Pipart Kawasaki. Notice how the rear brake master cylinder has a remote reservoir, tucked safely out of the way, and the quick-fill sump cap**

Below **An alternative method is the one used on this Nico Bakker chassis, in which a shackle operates a bell-crank to compress the single, vertical suspension unit** *(photos by John Robinson)*

Above In this layout the shackle is adjustable and the relative lengths of the operating mechanism give further adjustment on top of the spring/damper internal adjustment
Opposite The Bimota frame has its swing-arm pivot co-axial with the gearbox sprocket, giving no changes in chain tension as the suspension moves

(photos by John Robinson)

was no longer in the plane affected by the wheel's runout. Ironically, what was a problem on motorcycles is said to have proved useful in car racing. The Le Mans Jaguars suffered drag from their disc brakes which inhibited top speed, particularly along the fast Mulsanne straight. By setting the wheels up with slightly more runout than would otherwise have been used, they made the discs knock the pads clear and removed the drag.

Offenstadt built a trailing link fork, with struts operating a single damper unit mounted above the wheel. On the light 350 cc machines he used, this would seem even less necessary than for the more powerful heavyweights. As an indication of what the constructors of these machines were up against, a 700 Yamaha, in 24-hour

trim, weighed 130 kg. The early RCB, with a similar power output to the Yamaha of 110 to 120 bhp, weighed 200 kg. With slightly less power, the Godier-Genoud Kawasakis were considerably lighter: at 167 kg, roughly the same as the V-twin Ducatis. A stock Z1000 roadster, giving around 80 bhp, weighs 245 kg dry.

As the machines developed and the chassis and tyres became able to handle more power, the performance levels went up. Detail design became more critical than ever before. New tyre designs gave the teams a choice of slick, intermediate or wet-weather tyres and, to get the most from these tyres, they had to be changed with the weather. If patterned tyres were used in the dry they would overheat and the tread would tend to lift off. This could even happen with the intermediate types on the faster circuits such as Spa. So they had to be able to change wheels as often as the weather demanded and as quickly as possible.

Other maintenance items were equally important. It costs a lot of horsepower and rider effort to shave a few seconds off lap times, yet a pit stop can waste all that time and more. Vulnerable parts needed to be protected – many machines used remote reservoirs and master cylinders for their hydraulics so that they wouldn't be

wiped out in a crash. Other parts were mounted so that they could be replaced as complete systems. There is no time for lengthy diagnosis in a pit stop; where things like electrical components were concerned, it was easier to have the whole lot mounted on a quickly-detachable panel so that in the event of a misfire or some similar problem, the mechanic would simply unplug the panel containing the rectifier, regulator, CDI unit, fuse and even the switches, and refit another one.

The extent to which chassis development is important can be gauged by the racers' attitude towards engine performance. They could quite easily lift the power levels by using bigger carburetters and more violent camshafts, which would give the engine a narrow power band and make it less easy to use. Given good enough riders, which teams like Honda undoubtedly had, there wouldn't be a great problem in living with such a machine. Yet they opted for softer cams and Honda even used CV carburetters in order to keep flexibility, good fuel consumption and easy starting. If that is so important, it follows that any improvement in rider comfort is equally important.

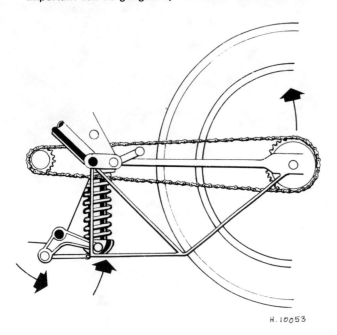

H.10053

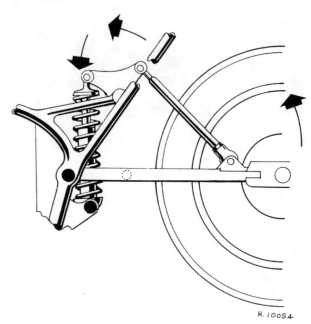

H.10054

Top left Operation of the Godier-Genoud rear suspension. The swing arm was triangulated, enabling it to be made of light tubing without losing strength. The lowest end was connected to a bell-crank which pivoted so as to compress a single spring/damper unit. A chain tensioner ran above the top of the swing-arm

Top right A similar arrangement is used in other types, including those made by Nico Bakker, except that the linkage is inverted with the bell-crank above the suspension unit and the swing-arm members working in compression instead of tension. This system, like the Godier-Genoud type offers a wide scope for adjustment. The spring/damper unit has provision for altering the spring rate, spring pre-load and damper force on bump and rebound. The linkage also permits the wheel rate and the ride height to be adjusted

Right A simpler, less sophisticated method is to use the triangulated swing-arm to compress the damper directly. This gives strength and simplicity but less scope for adjustment

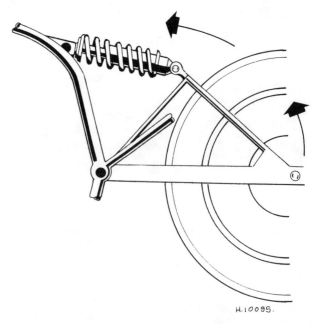

H.10095.

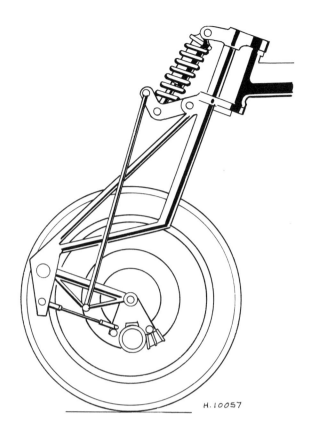

H.10057

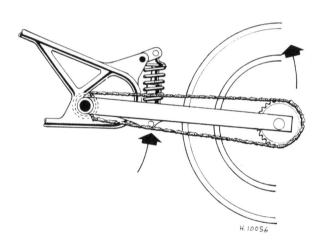

H.10056

Top Very few racers have deemed it necessary to go away from telescopic front forks. Mead and Tomkinson use hub-centre steering, the Gus Kuhn machine had leading link forks for one season and Eric Offenstadt produced these trailing link forks. The link pivots on a triangulated fork, using struts and bellcranks to compress a single de Carbon damper. The advantages are a high strength to weight ratio, quick wheel rate and ride height adjustment and more control over steering variations with suspension movement

Bottom One of the few systems which do not cause any changes in chain tension. On the Bimota chassis, the swing-arm pivots on the axis of the gearbox sprocket, so whatever position the wheel is in, chain tension remains constant. The arm also compresses a single, central damper. This layout demands a long swing-arm and a wide frame which hinders access to the gearbox and needs to be heavily braced

Chapter Five
Only as good as the rider?

Endurance racing has always been a feat — often of epic proportions — but originally it was seen as a contest between the rider and the elements, his fellow riders, and even his machine. The emphasis was purely on the rider's ability to keep going, and to keep his machine going, against all the odds. It was the rider — in the singular — who counted, and only one man was allowed to ride each machine.

Long-distance circuit races were conceived more or less as an athletic event in which the motorcycle was a necessary part of the apparatus, like a gymnast's parallel bars or a vaulter's pole. This distinguished the motorcycle races even from similar car marathons, where co-drivers were permitted. At the Le Mans 24-hour car race, which began a year after the Bol d'Or, two drivers took it in turns to handle their car.

This probably came about because the long circuit races evolved from marathon cross-country events and while a car could carry a passenger, who could obviously take the wheel to give the driver a break, this was not so easy in the equivalent motorcycle races.

The rules for the early Bol d'Or races set down the level of performance which the rider had to meet in order to qualify for inclusion in the results. During the first few hours he had to cover a minimum distance, according to the size of his machine. After that he was permitted rest periods as long as they didn't exceed a certain total. In modern events the same sort of thinking applies, a typical qualification rule being that the machine must complete 75 per cent of the race-winner's distance.

The disadvantages of the one-rider rule were seen early on but they were not argued from a safety angle. The main cause for concern was that one rider was not able to keep his machine going as hard as it could go and that the number of retirements from fatigue were in the same order as those caused by mechanical failures or crashes. It is possible that some of the crashes were caused by rider fatigue, of course, but that was accepted as part of the challenge. From the safety angle, there doesn't appear to have been any cause for concern. Even today, although two riders share each bike, fatigue is still one of the obstacles. Despite this, and the facts that the machines are nearly as rapid as Grand Prix racers and cover enormous racing mileages, the safety record must be one of the best in any form of motor racing. With any-

thing up to 80 entrants and race distances ranging from 500 to 3,000 miles, there have been remarkably few serious injuries.

Nevertheless, the crux of the matter was that, to judge the performance of the riders fairly, machines would be needed which were similar enough not to give anyone an advantage. And yet it was obvious after the first few races that slight modifications to the bikes and pit stop facilities could make big differences. There was never any suggestion that the machines should be subjected to rigid rules to ensure equality but the one man—one bike rule also held — right through to 1954.

The machine had long since become an integral part of the *team*, but when the rule was finally altered it was, initially, to allow the option of a co-rider. Even then, some stalwarts insisted on going ahead on their own.

Quite obviously, machine developments can affect the overall performance as much as the rider's skill and in long-distance races there are many factors which count equally with sheer speed. One approach would be to insist that all bikes should be identical, so that machines would revert to the role of athletic apparatus, and the racing would concentrate on selecting the rider with the most ability.

But endurance racing evolved in a way which encouraged machine development — and variety — until it reached the point where the bike was the spearhead of the *team*. Obviously the riders were as important as ever, but success depended on the smooth, efficient co-ordination of the whole team. The performance of a mechanic could gain or lose time; the judgements and decisions of a team manager could make the difference between winning, or not even finishing the race.

This makes endurance racing different from other types of event and is one of its attractions. But in a way it is also a disadvantage. From the rider's point of view, there are too many variables, any of which can cause problems.

Many world-class riders will not willingly take part in such events because — by definition — they are individualists to a high degree. Often helping with machine preparation, they are willing to work flat out during and in-between races. They will put 100 per cent effort into the racing and in return they ask for 100 per cent of the glory. They don't want to share either the riding or the winner's rostrum. This isn't a selfish attitude, but simply that, while they are prepared to make supreme efforts, they do not want to ask, or to rely on, anyone else to do the same. And conserving energy, instead of letting it all go in one enormous effort, is not part of a Grand Prix

Opposite **1976 — the contrast between the reigning champion, the Godier-Genoud Kawasaki and the contender, Honda's RCB** *(photo by Motorcycle Mechanics)*

Only as good as the rider?

rider's make-up. It is one thing to take calculated chances and get out in front, with a chequered flag as an immediate goal. It's an entirely different matter to pull out onto a circuit, into a stream of machines already thundering past at full speed, where the rider right in front of you may be 50 or 60 miles ahead in the race.

This is a loss to endurance racing and one more criticism follows from it — that the best riders are not taking part. In some ways this is valid, because when world-class riders do take part, they have little trouble in getting to the front. However, many such riders have been involved, especially since the early '70s. People like

Ken Hull fires up the Honda Britain RCB in the Brands Hatch pit road

(photo by John Robinson)

Smart, Pickrell, Jefferies, several Williamses (Charlie, John and Peter), George, Mortimer, Rutter and Read from the UK and continental stars like Pons, Sarron and Lucchinelli — I'd rather not attempt to make an exhaustive list for fear of leaving someone out. The point is that riders of this calibre have been drawn into the endurance events with the immediate result that the level of competition was raised. And many of them took a liking to it and came back.

Even then, it wasn't a case of the established stars blowing everyone else into the weeds. As long-distance racing progressed, specialist teams evolved with highly specialised equipment and refined back-up services. It was difficult to gauge the ability of many of the riders, because they concentrated on this kind of racing and didn't appear in the Grand Prix circus. But when endurance racing became important enough to attract

the established stars, they were up against the specialists and the racing was never exactly one-sided.

On the Continent and particularly in France, endurance racing has enjoyed a lot of prestige and popularity. Large prizes were augmented by newspaper, radio and television coverage plus, of course, detailed reports in the specialist press. So the events attracted many riders who might otherwise have made a name for themselves in Grands Prix.

The overall result has been seen in a very high standard of riding, some exciting high-speed demonstrations and not a few surprises. The growing prestige and prize money were not totally unconnected with the riders' attitudes but an ace rider could no longer rely on his own abilities.

Yvon Duhamel put in regular appearances at Le Mans, riding the Godier Kawasaki with Jean-Francois

Baldé. Duhamel knows only one way to ride, be it short-circuit, snowmobile or 24-hour racing, and in his attempts to get in front he would fall off fairly regularly. His answer was to go faster still to make up for the time lost in wearing his leathers out, and the result was often spectacular. But he was being beaten by the specialists — including team-mates Godier and Genoud in '75 and, in '76, by the works Honda ridden by Chemarin and another Grand Prix rider, Alex George, who replaced the injured Christian Léon.

The only other way to evaluate the performance of the endurance teams is to compare lap times with the GP

Fast, consistent, a race-school instructor at Le Mans, Jean-Claude Chemarin made it his business not to make mistakes *(photo by John Robinson)*

Only as good as the rider?

bikes on the same circuits. Often the endurance machines get within a few seconds of the 500cc lap record and occasionally, such as at the Nürburgring, they beat the lap record. Admittedly they have bigger engines but they carry more equipment and the riders are mentally pacing themselves for long, tiring races.

In some events there are real advantages in keeping up a high pace. Psychologically it helps the team's morale – and detunes the opposition – which is one tactic favoured by the French Honda riders. Léon and Chemarin have a reputation of being the team to beat and they keep up this pressure even in practice. The 1977 Spa 24-

Even faster but more prone to the odd crash, Christian Léon became the man to beat

(photo by John Robinson)

hour race was a typical example. Although rapidly-changing weather added a lot of uncertainty to the official practice periods, the French riders were one of the few teams to go out on slick tyres. The circuit was misty in places and there were damp patches left from the last shower but as soon as they thought the weather looked bright enough they loaded up slicks and Léon went out to see what he could do. The result was a lap some four seconds quicker than the next fastest machine – a Kawasaki running on intermediate tyres.

During the races there is no question of settling down to an easy pace – they race all the way. 'Easing off' merely means that a rider is being careful not to let the engine over-rev and not to take chances in corners. He has to offset the potential gain of a few tenths of a second against the loss of many minutes in repairing a crashed bike. But for the leading machines there are

reasons for pressing on in the early stages of the race. There will probably be awards for the leader at the end of each hour or for the best performance during the hour. There will be valuable publicity from the late evening and early morning news reports. And better still, there will be the pressure on the following bikes; those who are on possibly quicker machines but are down in fifth or sixth place, probably because they made a small error. Perhaps they overshot a corner, or the bike wouldn't fire up after a pit stop. Whatever the reason, the pressure is on them to catch up and that is when they are more likely to make another mistake.

Those are the sort of tactics the teams use. If it was ever a game of cat and mouse, the mouse has now got nowhere to hide.

Time and again, the specialists have proved their point: that riding ability and machine performance are not the only factors that make the difference between winning and losing. Look at it this way — if you rode an ordinary bike for 24 hours, you'd have to stop for fuel maybe a dozen times. Without quick-fill tanks, that might cost 20 to 30 minutes and you could allow anything up to another 30 minutes for repairs, maintenance, and tyre and brake changes. You might end up riding for only 23 out of 24 hours, and if you can streamline your operation to cut into this 'dead' hour you can really gain time. If, however, you decide to scratch around the circuit you might shave 1 or 2 seconds off a lap time of, say, 2

Charlie Williams, preferred endurance racing to short circuits, and partnered by Stan Woods, the British team could equal the performances of the French Honda riders *(photo by John Robinson)*

Only as good as the rider?

minutes. That's a gain of 1 minute for every hour and every extra effort brings you that much closer to a crash or a mechanical failure. Logically, there is more to be gained by shaving time off the pit stops. The best teams do *both*.

There is still room for further development and improvement, though. The quickest teams take something like five or six seconds to refuel, while changing both wheels takes something in the order of 30 seconds to 1 minute. The 1978 Lotus Formula One team could change all four of their wheels in 13 seconds.

Jacques Luc shows off his neat, smooth style in Paul Ricard's sweeping curves. His impeccable riding won him victories at the demanding Spa-Francorchamps circuit *(photo by John Robinson)*

Many of the riders go as hard as they would in a 40-minute race and the only trick here is in choosing a rider who can keep that up for the full distance without falling off. The machines have reached the stage of reliability where they can cope mechanically and the pit crews are carefully rehearsed in the routine stops. Problems arise when something unusual happens — a crash which could cause all manner of misleading after–effects as well as the obvious damage. Sand in the carburetters or damaged wiring can take a lot of time to trace and rectify. Diagnosing an elusive fault is also time-consuming; the bikes are built so that complete systems can be changed quickly and the most important thing, generally, is to keep the machine moving. Often it's a question of taking an educated guess at the fault, changing the offending item and getting the bike back on the circuit, hoping that it won't come back into the pits on the next lap.

Problems like this have more far-reaching effects; they disturb the rhythm of the team and they put the riders and mechanics on a very sharp edge. It's not easy for a mechanic to sit back and think, when everyone around expects him to be *doing* something. So the mechanics have got to be fast and accurate – and good enough for the riders to have confidence in them. More than that, everyone in the team needs the right sort of personality to cope with these mounting problems without losing their temper or their concentration.

Circuits like Spa make any problems worse still. The sheer speed stresses the machine and riders to an intense level, with the variable weather thrown in to make matters worse. On a normal short circuit, the rider has a fair chance of being able to push a broken bike back to the pits. With nearly nine miles at the Belgian track, the odds are definitely against him.

The 24-hour race here in 1977 highlighted just about all the problems that the endurance teams have to face. Christian Léon had done his demoralising act in practice and put the French Honda in pole position. The Honda France team had three machines entered, the other two being ridden by Korhonen/Huguet and Luc/Soulas. The Honda Britain team had Stan Woods and Charlie Williams riding a 77, with Tony Rutter and Roger Marshall on a 76.

Honda Britain's racing operation, under Gerald Davison, extended to Formula One events and, the same

Phil Read partnered Tony Rutter for the '77 Bol d'Or. A persistent oil leak lubricated the back tyre and hindered their progress

(photo by Rod Sloane)

weekend as the Spa race, Ron Haslam was having his first race for Honda at Silverstone. Alf Briggs was responsible for the pre-race preparation of the endurance racers, working with a team of full-time mechanics plus other assistants, including a doctor. Rather pedantic about detail organisation, Briggs is a reticent type who combines tidiness with technical knowledge and years of experience. While tending to keep out of the forefront of things he managed to keep the team quietly in control and produced logical order when many things started happening at the same time. He had organised the semi-official entries, based on the CB750, which were raced in the early '70s, and one of which won at Spa, ridden by Charlie Williams and John Williams. In contrast to the boisterous and sometimes cynical riders, Briggs was a quiet introvert but an ideal choice for team manager. His experience and value to the team were more than apparent in the way the riders respected his decisions — even in casual conversation they would refer to him as Mr. Briggs.

The weather leading up to the start of the 1977 race had caused plenty of uncertainty about tyres, some riders using slicks, and others opting for intermediate tyres. At 400 rpm Korhonen shot away from the Le Mans-type start, heeling the screaming RCB left and then right through the uphill sweep away from the start straight. Slick tyres are unpredictable before they've warmed up,

but Korhonen's Honda, closely followed by the Léon/Chemarin machine, made it obvious that the French were going to make the most of the dry roads before the next shower.

The problems started within minutes of the start. Stan Woods appeared, travelling slowly, wobbling around the hairpin and down into the pit road with the bike bumping on a back tyre which was breaking up.

Other bikes followed with the same problem, caused by the tyres overheating or perhaps a faulty batch of tyres. Then it rained and the frantic search for more tyres was complicated by the machines coming in to have patterned tyres fitted. Because of the high speed and bumpy roads, it was possible that the tyre was fouling on the seat, so the Honda Britain team fitted longer suspen-

Opposite top **The heavily braced frame used on the Dholda RCB. The attention to detail is typical: locking wire and springs on the chassis fittings, Dzus fasteners on the fairing mounts, the additional brake bleed nipple mounted above the master cylinder**
Opposite bottom **Pre-race preparation reveals the detail construction of this Harris-framed Kawasaki**
Below **Quick-fill dump tanks lined up along the pit road at Paul Ricard**

(photos by John Robinson)

Only as good as the rider?

sion legs. The 76 bike was up to third place behind the French Hondas but when it came in they noticed that the rear brake line had been damaged. Removing the whole system took only a matter of minutes but while the 76 was still in the pits, the 77 made an unscheduled stop, spluttering in with a misfire.

With no time for diagnosis, the best plan was to

Opposite **An endless job for the tyre-fitters – and a picture which sums up the problems facing the riders at Spa. Slicks, intermediate and wet weather tyres might be needed in quick succession**
Below **Refuelling isn't without its problems. Jacques Luc waits to take over his Godier-Genoud Kawasaki as the mechanics demonstrate their quick-spiller**
(photos by Motorcycle Mechanics)

change the easiest item, refuel the bike and see if it went. The CDI unit was replaced, the bike fired up and Woods took it back into the race. By this time the Léon/Chemarin bike had caught the leading Honda, but the British RCBs had lost several places. Once both bikes were running there was time to work out possible solutions if the misfire returned. It had happened as the fuel level got low in the tank, and, as they'd had problems with the tank valves, a spare tank was checked over and made ready for fitting at the next stop. Within an hour – before schedule – Woods was back and so was the misfire. The new tank was fitted as a precaution, although Woods had already tried opening the top filler cap to eliminate the possibility of an air lock. The riders had reported a misfire during practice but, surprisingly, the fault had not been located. Afterwards, a bent magneto armature was diagnosed, although this didn't explain the intermittent

Only as good as the rider?

nature of the misfire. Coming on top of the tyre and weather problems, it put a big strain on the team's morale. They knew there was a fault and they knew that there shouldn't be. But they didn't know who – if anyone – the fault belonged to.

The next casualty was the 76, with a broken seat, which was patched up to keep the bike moving and give the mechanics time to make up metal struts to reinforce the seats of both machines. These were fitted as the bikes came in for fuelling.

The British bikes were beginning to move up through the field, although the misfire persisted as the tank emptied. By midnight they had progressively changed

virtually everything that could cause the problem: the ignition system, the plugs, the coils, even the tank and the carburetters, all to no avail. Other teams were having similar problems and it seemed possible that fuel surge combined with the necessarily high flow rate at high speeds was causing fuel starvation. They decided to live with it, bringing the bike in for refuelling earlier.

Problems with the British Honda also caused trouble for the leading French bike. During the night, Chemarin had tucked in behind Williams, not realising that the RCB would slow down as the misfire set in. In a long, normally fast, left-hand curve, the RCB began spluttering and then suddenly accelerated as Chemarin ran into the back of it. Williams managed to keep control, but the French rider came off and Phil Carpenter, close behind on the Mead and Tomkinson Kawasaki, hit the wreckage. Carpenter spent the night in the local hospital and Chemarin, uninjured, had to push his RCB a mile or so to the pits, with a

After eleven hours of racing ... the leaderboard at Montjuich Park tells it all

(photo by Motorcycle Mechanics)

wrecked front end. That took half an hour, and it took the mechanics another 45 minutes to strip out the forks, wheel, brake and oil cooler and replace them with parts from a spare machine.

By the time Léon took the bike out again, they had dropped from first place right down the field. The French bike had also been suffering from a misfire and they were running it with the reserve tap open. This was one solution which Briggs had decided not to try. Towards the end of its stint, the RCB disappeared – Léon was pushing it back in with an empty fuel tank. Huguet had also crashed, leaving the Luc/Soulas RCB in the lead and – by the time Léon had got back and refuelled – it was some 180 miles in front of Léon/Chemarin.

The British bikes were circulating steadily – and then the 76 disappeared altogether. It had stopped with an engine failure, miles away on the far side of the circuit. As Chemarin worked his way up into 10th spot, Stan Woods was keeping the 77 in 5th place – all he needed to get a points lead in the Endurance Championship – and had

settled down to a steady ride to the finish. The French team were still racing, though.

At 1pm, there was the Luc/Soulas Honda well out in front, and the British Honda still fifth. A few minutes later the Léon/Chemarin RCB slipped past the British bike into 5th place. At 1.30 it rained, slowing the bikes down but the French team decided to keep on taking chances and at 2.00 pm they moved into 4th place. By 3.00 pm, with one hour left, they had taken 3rd place, behind the German Meyer Honda. There was no hope of catching their team-mates on the first bike, but in front of a delirious crowd Léon passed the German rider on the last lap, to take second place.

The kind of pitwork that each team has to face had literally plagued both French and British teams during the race. Yet despite the inspired performance by Léon and Chemarin, they were unable to make up for the smooth riding and lack of trouble which distinguished the winning Luc/Soulas partnership.

Chapter Six
Atmosphere

At an endurance race it isn't uncommon to see perhaps twenty different types of machine plus untold variations based on the theme of the Kawasaki and Honda fours. The only other type of road racing which offers such variety is production racing but that lacks the innovation of the special builders, the noise and the sheer performance of racing machines.

Long-distance racing reached something of a peak when the SIDEMM Kawasakis were at their best and the works Hondas were beginning to get under way. This coincided with a boom in motorcycling generally and the organisers of the events were able to cash in on the sudden popularity which they did in quite a shrewd manner. Realising that a long race won't hold the attention of spectators for its full duration, side attractions were laid on and probably none were quite so comprehensive or as lavish as those at the Bol d'Or. After several years at Le Mans, the Bol d'Or was switched to the Paul Ricard circuit in 1978 (with a separate 24-hour race at Le Mans earlier in the year) and the organisers were able to announce a four-day carnival of motorcycling.

The two French 24-hour events also catered for production-type machines. At Le Mans there were classes for 'silhouettes' as well as prototypes, while at the Bol d'Or there was a separate race, the Bol d'Argent, catering for strictly production machines. Faced with a sudden decline in motorcycling, or a change in the rules governing endurance racing, the Bol d'Or has, like the TT before it, established itself as an event in its own right, to which the faithful will continue to make their annual pilgrimage.

In its new location in the South of France, the Bol d'Or could also guarantee weather to match the social occasion, far from the traditional rain which was a part of Le Mans. Starting on a Thursday with scrutineering for the machines, there was practice for the endurance bikes plus the other classes in the supporting races. Traditionally the supporting races have always been the opposite of the big endurance specials, with production 400 Kawasakis and 125 Motobécanes. In 1978, more events were added; there were 250 and 750 French National Championships, the Challenge Honda for 125 four-strokes, and the six-hour production race.

On Friday there was more practice, and the start of the Bol d'Argent, running from 6 pm through until midnight, being, incidentally, the first European race to see the new Japanese machines such as the Honda CBX and the Yamaha XS1100.

Paul Ricard is a purpose-built circuit and the visitor gets a hint of the facilities at the wide entrance area, with its underpass leading off the public road. After passing an enduro training ground and camping areas, there is a rocky trials course and a llimpse of an airstrip before the colourful towers and marquees of the circuit itself. The track is laid out for safety as well as spectator visibility, with steep banks or grandstands in all the public areas. There is a wide verge following the circuit, with run-off areas and safety fences on the corners.

To add to the racing, a whole range of side-attractions, typical of the village at Le Mans, were set up around the track, with closed circuit television monitors keeping everyone in touch with the racing, latest results and interviews.

The Tasse d'Or was a sort of rally which laid on special rail excursions, camping and so on, to help youngsters, who normally rely on mopeds, to get to the far south. Continental circuits differ from those in the UK in that they are geared up to high entrance prices but once inside there are no further charges; even the programmes are free as are most of the sideshows offering amusing diversions.

One of these was a museum of famous motorcycles including models such as the four-valve Rudge, model 90 Sunbeam and KTT Velocette; from France the 250 Terrot and 350 Jonghi; the Belgian FN and Saroléa; the Italian 500 Guzzi, 125 Rumi and 250 Parilla; the German 125 DKW and the 250 and 500 NSU.

At the trials course there were demonstrations by National experts and, for those who brought their own machines, free practice and tuition. During the preamble leading up to the major event there were demonstrations of trick riding by trial stars, including the American Debbie Evans, showing off her skills in Europe for the first time.

Around the perimeter of the circuit there were ample camp sites, unfortunately labelled and signposted 'Concentration', but that didn't seem to put anyone off. Several groups of enthusiasts, one-make clubs and so on, had commandeered sites for rally-like gatherings.

As well as permanent bars and restaurants within the circuit buildings, many stalls had appeared offering the Gallic equivalents of hotdogs – chips, waffles, pancakes and roast chicken. All around were signs of carnival time,

Opposite **The carnival of the Bol d'Or is backed up by the traditional 'boys' race – contenders for the Coupe Kawasaki ease their 400s through the slipper S-curves at Le Mans** *(photo by Motorcycle Mechanics)*

Atmosphere

the funfair, an open-air big-screen cinema, karting circuit and stalls and stands displaying motorcycling clothing and accessories. Further around the circuit there was a motocross track, where events would be run during the main race. To round off the amusements, there was even a bullring.

During practice days there was always something going on – as soon as bikes had vacated the track, it would be occupied by a film crew, using one of the well-known riders with a camera mounted on his machine, while another crew would be filming one of the racers as the seat, tank and other ancillaries were removed.

Some weren't so lucky ... the supporting races are as closely-fought as any grand prix
(photo by Motorcycle Mechanics)

At the end of practice on that Friday in 1978, the officially-timed qualifying laps had been made and the pace of the bikes could be seen. Way out in front, the specially prepared OW31, ridden by Pons and Sarron, was obviously much faster than the bigger, heavier four-strokes. Every year someone turns up with a GP Yamaha but, as everyone was explaining to everyone else, they never made it to the finish. Maybe this year ... at least there were half a dozen Yamaha OW31s entered plus a couple of TZ350s. Another novelty was the number of machines using two-way radio – a couple in the Bol d'Or and a couple more in the Bol d'Argent, which started at 6 pm on Friday.

There were over 100 entries for this production race including several CBX Hondas and some XS1100 Yamahas, plus the inevitable 1000 cc Kawasakis. The smallest bikes were 350s and 400s but all were meant to

conform strictly to showroom specification. The prize money suggested that competition would be fierce — 10,000F for the winner, going down progressively to 500F for 10th place, 400F for 11th to 20th, and 200F for all finishers. The French Foreign Legion had donated a prize of 200F for the leading team at the end of each hour.

The race ended at midnight and was eventually won by a Honda CBX, although the surprise was a Z650 Kawasaki, which was always among the first three. This completely stock machine was quite happily blowing-off the one-litre bikes all around the circuit.

All day, enthusiasts had been pouring in from all over Europe, many having started some 500 or more miles away in the cold, wet North. In the bright heat of the Southern hills, bikes were now rolling in with all the superfluous clothing stacked precariously on top of the camping gear. Towns and villages for miles around swarmed with motorcycles and their attendant paraphernalia. The winding alpine roads leading from the Haute Savoie to the Alpes Maritimes echoed to the screams of replacement exhausts.

The next day, Saturday, was like all the days before: bright enough to send British photographers looking for slower films, and hot. It was also race-day and things got off to a prompt start at 8.30 a.m. While the crowds built up at the entrance booths and the entrenched campers wondered why they'd brought glass-fibre-lined suits, the first crackles of racing exhausts sounded the start of the

The sheer size and elaborate modification of the endurance racers makes a stark contrast with the production Kawasakis *(photo by Motorcycle Mechanics)*

Trophée Savoye. This seven-lap race for 125 cc Moto Aspes machines was typical of the build-up to the Bol d'Or.

Just as the race itself thrives on paradox – roadsters turned into racers, fairly equal competition between big and small – so the supporting races tend to be diametrically opposed to the main event. After the 125s, there was the traditional Coupe Kawasaki. This 8-lap race is part of a national series for up-and-coming French youngsters. They ride production 400 Kawasakis, fitted with fairings, clip-ons, rear-set footrests and raised exhausts; otherwise the machines are completely standard.

The equality of the machines ensures very close competition and the riders, in front of crowds of International proportions, are stimulated to great efforts. From the original 'boy's race', set up as an amusing diversion, the Coupe Kawasaki has acquired a prestige of its own. Emulated in Belgium (and later in the UK), it has also inspired a further event which is run annually at the Bol d'Or, with a team of the best Belgian riders versus a team from France.

The racing is taken seriously, by the riders and by the crowds, and quite a few of France's top-line racers, such as Pons, Sarron and Boulom, are 'graduates' of the Coupe Kawasaki.

Another, similar event, was next on the agenda – the Challenge Honda, similar to the 125 series held in the UK but running four-stroke singles instead of the two-stroke engines. The popularity of these races can be gauged by the entry – around 80 riders for both the Coupe Kawasaki and Trophée Savoye, and over 200 for the Challenge Honda. At Paul Ricard the organisers succeeded in a difficult task – they had combined a prestigious 24-hour race with the fast-moving programme of a short-circuit meeting and, of course, the whole carnival which is the Bol d'Or. And by this time it was still only 10 am!

A new angle was introduced at the '78 race, the inclusion of French National Championship events, for 250 and 750 classes. This took the racing up to midday, just as the ceremony leading to the start of the 24-hour race was building up.

Along the pit straight the trials experts performed some unlikely balancing acts and a team of stunt drivers raced their cars back and forth, mainly on two wheels. Gradually the endurance racers were made ready, in time for a final exhibition as all the machines were wheeled out into their starting positions.

There were the RCBs, of course – official entries from France, Britain, Holland, Germany, Belgium and even Brazil; the high-revving special motor built by Honda NR to be ridden by the Americans Emde and Klinzman; and other RCBs used by Dholda and Japauto. Other Honda machines were entered, although not so many as in previous years, the most 'different' one being a standard-looking CBX which was alleged to have a works-prepared engine.

There were more signs of the new generation bikes creeping in, a couple of XS1100 Yamahas and a GS1000 Suzuki, all unfaired and looking pretty much as the factory had intended. The Suzuki though, which had been taken out to 1100 cc, came with Pops Yoshimura attending it and riders Pierce and Cooley – who had the distinction of beating the Hondas on home ground, in the 8-hour race held at Japan's Suzuka circuit. The Suzuki proved to be surprisingly quick during the early stages of the race, but was put out of the running by a failure in the ignition rotor.

To complete the four-cylinder Japanese line-up, there were any number of big Kawasakis. Kool cigarettes had sponsored a team of five, four basically standard machines bored to 1100 cc and one Pipart Kawasaki, with a cantilever frame and two-way radio.

Other Kawasaki variants differed mainly in their chassis: the National Moto machines, with conventional swinging arm (controlled by one massive damper) Bimota frames, the orthodox Peckett and McNab bikes, Martin Kawasakis and, going right away from convention, the still-developing Mead and Tomkinson bike.

Apart from the Yamahas, the only small engine was that in a Laverda 500 twin, backed up by 1000 cc machines from the same factory, including their prototype – in the truest sense of the word. This was the shaft-drive, watercooled V-6, being developed specifically as an endurance racer because this was the only type of racing that encouraged machines on which future roadsters might be based.

Other European manufacturers were represented, but not in an official capacity, by a smattering of Guzzis, BMWs, Ducatis and a lone 750 Triumph.

At 4 pm the riders were lined up opposite their machines for the traditional Le Mans start. They sprint across to the bikes, engines dead, fire them up and get away as fast as they can. This type of start has been criticised – and it usually looks hairy enough – but in practice there are no more incidents than those caused by clutch starts, and this is the only practical alternative. Rolling starts, controlled by a pace car, have been tried and do offer the advantage of a warm-up lap but there are problems. The pace and timing have to be carefully controlled – the procession can string out and, as the

Opposite top **In '78 the Bol d'Or moved to the purpose-built Ricard circuit in the South of France. Its never-ending series of curves are lined with wide run-off areas and catch fences**
Opposite bottom **The sun rises on an abandonned Guzzi standing idle at the trackside, but the racing goes on** *(photos by John Robinson)*

Atmosphere

pace car ducks out of the way, the tail end bikes can be travelling much faster than those in front, resulting in tight bunching and a lot of crowding as the pack get into the first turn.

Not unexpectedly, the Pons/Sarron Sonauto Yamaha soon got into the lead. This OW31 had been carefully prepared, just for the Bol d'Or. The highly experienced Christian Maingret reworked the watercooled two-stroke into endurance trim mainly by aiming to make it reliable and to streamline the necessarily frequent pit stops. The Yamaha was covered in quick-change items, from the

The Peyre/Maingret Pipart Kawasaki pushes Stan Woods on the British Honda. The RCB was third and the Kawasaki fourth

(photo by John Robinson)

fairing through to its battery which, with no generator, had to be changed at each night-time fuelling stop. The speed and handling of the light racer soon made itself felt and, from the trackside, it was easy to identify the Yamaha purely from its speed and angle of bank in the corners.

But it wasn't having things all its own way. The Léon/Chemarin RCB was right behind, followed by the 1100 Suzuki. The racing was so close that at the end of the first hour, all three bikes were on the same lap. As the bikes took on fuel and changed riders, it became obvious that Maingret had got his sums right – the Yamaha got the lead and kept it, regularly putting in the best hourly performance and not letting its high fuel consumption or lack of a generator hinder its progress. This was worthwhile in itself, as there was a prize of 1,000F for the greatest distance covered in each hour, plus 5,000F for

the best performance in any one hour. The Yamaha scooped this bonus as well as staying in the lead for 17 hours until, to the relief of those who make predictions, its crankshaft failed.

While the racing got under way, the sideshows swung into action; up above, nine Magisters of la Patrouille de France were flying as close together as they dared without doubling their insurance premium; around the back of the circuit, fifty riders were pitting their 125 Yamahas in a motocross; over to one side, BMW unveiled their new 450 and 650 models to the public and a rock band were warming up their amplifiers, while the racers continued to battle for the 50,000F prize.

Once again Honda took the first three places, Chemarin, on the winning bike, making it three Bols in a row. Traditions have grown in the Bol d'Or — as the clock moves around to 24th hour, crowds defy the fencing and the cordon of gendarmerie, spilling onto the track to greet the finishers.

If the leading bikes are far enough ahead to be safe, team riders group up, thundering past the crowd in formation and often, towards the final lap, slowing to stay behind riders struggling with a sick machine.

But in '78 the crowd overdid things, getting too close for safety, if not comfort, and the chequered flag appeared several minutes before the 24 hours were up.

As the 1978 Bol ended, so did an era of endurance racing. Honda, with nothing left to win, had already set their sights on the 500 cc World Championship. Their

Hubert Rigal wearily pushes into the pits, after crashing when his Honda's front tyre punctured

(photo by Rod Sloane)

Atmosphere

RCBs had done all that was wanted of them; further development would not be easy and, more to the point, would not be necessary. In the chase after the works Hondas, the Kawasakis had become exhausted. No other manufacturer would take on Honda on these terms — not once Honda had a three year start. And the privateers lacked the basic machinery.

Without Honda, the privateers will once again be able to fight it out amongst themselves. And other factories might see an opportunity of doing what Honda did. There's plenty of raw material for a fresh start. The new roadster Suzuki, Yamaha and Honda with four and six cylinder configurations have plenty of potential. Other factories such as Laverda either have suitable prototypes or the means to produce them. And, to some extent, the need to build them — with the exception of Laverdà, none of the European factories have had a new design in the last five years.

Formula One is currently where F750 was in the days of the Tridents. It's not that the Formula racers have superficial similarities to the endurance machines — in fact it wouldn't be too easy to convert one into the other. But factories supporting F1 will probably produce developments which will be useful in endurance, just as F750 did some years ago. It's of passing interest that the 1978 F1 TT-winning Ducati, used by Hailwood, was descended from the 1973 prototype which won at Barcelona.

The success of F1 may bring a forced coming-together of the two types of racing — if the FIM decide to make another World Championship out of endurance racing and if they decide to restrict it with a Formula. The FIM has often demonstrated its inability to make logical decisions, so predictions are largely a waste of time.

All that is predictable is that endurance racers will be based on big roadsters as far as privateers are concerned. Where the factories are concerned there is still hope for genuine prototypes upon which future roadsters will be based.

A typical end to 24 hours of racing, the crowd slowly edges onto the track awaiting the winner
(photo by Motorcycling Mechanics)

Chapter Seven
Factory support

Since the earliest races manufacturers have seen, and used, the advantages of publicising their sporting achievements. While the implication of such advertisement is that the manufacturer can make a product which is better than those made by his competitors, the theme has usually been that the self-same product is available to the customers.

Although the types of machines and even the type of racing have changed over the years, works' involvement in racing always follows the same pattern. Initial successes are followed by further development and modifications to the machine. The success and valuable publicity achieved by this work encourage the manufacturer to get more deeply involved. Modifications are incorporated into the next batch of roadsters, or works 'replica' machines are made available, although these are obviously one step behind the factory models.

Eventually this leads to a saturation point in development and, where a machine has been particularly successful, it will have removed most of the competition from its class. Typical examples of this saturation level are the Manx Norton, the Gold Star and, more recently the 350 Yamaha twins. When this level is reached, nearly everyone will be riding the model concerned and apart from the fact that there is no development left in the machine, there is no point in the manufacturer competing against himself. An alternative is that the class of racing may be changed, or someone else will come along with a

Barcelona 1972, the final fling of the Spanish factory lightweights. After years of success, the single cylinder two-stroke Bultaco had grown to 360cc
(photo by Motorcycling Mechanics)

Factory support

brand new machine, and the original bike will become obsolete. Unless the manufacturer has also got something new up his sleeve, his best plan is to get out of racing. Occasionally more than one manufacturer has been involved and the result has been high-speed development and a total commitment to a full Grand Prix development programme. This happened with Honda, Suzuki and Yamaha in the '60s — but eventually it gets too expensive. The publicity value and the sales of new machines cease to justify the expense of competition and the manufacturers pull out.

The course of events is always the same: fierce competition, an exciting level of development which gradually tails off to a saturation — and stagnation — point. The racing world then marks time, with privateers having a field day, until the next manufacturer comes up with the goods.

The stakes — and the pace — are higher in GP racing, but production racing goes through the same cycles. In the '20s and '30s there was, on the whole, a smaller difference between race bikes and production models. An individual could buy models such as the KTT Velocette, with modifications representing the previous year's works machines. Even the touring KSS model wasn't so far removed from the basic design. So racing models could be seen to be based on what was available in the showrooms, and touring models enjoyed the benefits of

A lot of effort went into the chassis design of the Norton twins, starting with the Norvil production racer and going through to the monocoque chassis. Here Peter Williams tries the cantilever suspension model *(photo by Motorcycle Mechanics)*

racing successes. Later on production racing, and particularly endurance racing, changed so that manufacturers with no GP machines could still enter their sports models and sports prototypes. This 'sports' category eventually became a euphemism for racing machines, with all the attendant development and glory.

The long-distance races, of course, have always been an ideal place for a manufacturer to demonstrate the speed and reliability of his models. Even where pure racers have been used, there is always the implication ... 'If we can make our racers so reliable, think how much more reliable our roadsters must be.'

After winning the 1922 Bol d'Or, Motosacoche were able to advertise their 500 as 'the machine which has proved, by its resounding victories, that it combines all the qualities necessary for the ideal vehicle'. Of course, a 24-hour race, with only one rider per machine, did

illustrate many qualities above and beyond mere speed.

In 1924, DFR were proclaiming their successes, with the comment that 'all these results were obtained with strictly standard machines.'

After World War II, the long-distance races provided the enthusiast with enjoyable events, where he could use his inexpensive lightweight and get more racing miles to his franc than anywhere else. Obviously it wasn't so attractive from a spectator's point of view but it was very good for small factories like Ossa, Montesa and Bultaco. With special versions of their bread-and-butter light-

BMWs have figured in endurance races regularly, with varying degrees of officialdom. Helmut Dahne shared this 980 Krauser BMW with Peter Zettelmeyer at the '76 Bol d'Or *(photo by Motorcycle Mechanics)*

weights, they could go racing without a huge budget *and* get publicity for it.

A prototype class was arranged for the Barcelona 24-hour event and, although the factories might have been racing on their own terms, their lightweight two-strokes were beating 650s.

Montesa started the ball rolling with a win at Barcelona, using an experimental 175. Bultaco, looking for publicity outside Spain to help their exports, built a 125 streamliner which they took to Montlhéry in 1960 for a world record attempt. They took the 24-hour world record for the 125 class and also beat the existing 250 and 350 records. Perhaps the publicity backfired on them, because Ducati also saw the advantages of the prototype class and went to Barcelona the same year with a 175. They won the race with it, finishing ahead of a 600 BMW. Then in 1962, a works Ducati won the 250

class, while a six-speed, watercooled Bultaco won the 125 class.

Bultaco's efforts reached a peak in '63, when a race-modified version of their Metralla model won the *Coupe d'Endurance.* Montesa kept their prestige with a local win at Barcelona. They were back in '64, managing a 250 class win and 3rd overall – the outright winner was once again a Ducati, a 285 cc model ridden by Spaggiari and Mandolini.

Ossa, contemplating an export drive, decided to use the Barcelona race to publicise their new prototype. This machine, a 175, won its class against Bultacos and Montesas, and was also raced at Thruxton where it came 6th in the 250 class.

A team of 250 Montesas were entered, but ironically a privately-entered Montesa beat them into second place, although the marque took the first three places in the 250 class.

The publicity was beginning to pay off. Just to prove that they meant business, Ossa had their 175 in production – and for export – in 1966. Meanwhile they were working on a new 230 cc prototype and had started making plans for a GP racer. The new machine managed

The biggest factory effort came from Honda in 1976 after tentative development work in '75 and earlier 'private' entries. This is the 76 RCB entered by Honda France *(photo by Motorcycle Mechanics)*

The Honda Britain team used a similar model – note the de Carbon dampers, Lockheed brakes and the CV carburetters *(photo by Honda UK)*

a 5th place overall at Barcelona and two works Montesa 250s took first and second place. British teams filled the gap, Phillips and Croxford sharing the third-place 500 Velocette, followed by Degens and Butcher on a 650 Triumph-powered Norton.

The performance of small bikes was proving quite useful elsewhere – a 250 Ducati won the 6-hour race at Imola, in a class catering for machines of up to 750 cc.

For 1967 Ossa continued their development and expansion. The 230 was in production and its already sporting specification could be uprated by an optional race-kit. Their machines came 11th in the Production TT and took the first two places overall at Barcelona. They had expanded the range of models, producing trials, motocross and enduro machines, one of which received a Gold medal in the Scottish Six Day Trial. The Grand Prix programme was also developing well enough for their rider, Santiago Herrero, to finish seventh in the 1968 250 cc World Championship. His machine was still a single-cylinder two-stroke, like all the other Ossa models. They also won the 250 Production TT but Ducati were still proving that the four-stroke single was a force to be reckoned with, winning the 250 class at Barcelona and finishing third overall.

In 1969, Herrero gave Ossa a third place in the 250 World Championship but tragedy struck the team the following year when he died after crashing in the TT. This brought the Spanish factory's racing plans to a premature close, but in endurance racing there were new models appearing which would drastically overshadow the small two-strokes.

A 360 Bultaco won the Barcelona race in the year that the 750 Triumph and Honda models started to hit the sales charts. Both of these factories were taking an interest in Daytona-type races and Ducati were about to bring forth their 750 V-twin, forerunner of the bikes which won at Imola and, in the hands of Ferrari and Grau, it made quite an impression in long-distance racing.

The Spanish factories had taken their basic, utility machines and turned them into successful racers. Development from there saw them increase from 125s, growing slowly into 360s some ten years later. Fortunately, just as they reached their saturation point as

Factory support

far as race development was concerned, a new generation of big bikes arrived to keep things going. The adaptability of the lively two-strokes allowed them to branch out into off-road sport and to go their own ways from there. Ducati, who had concentrated on four-stroke singles, doubled things up to produce their big V-twins and continued their interest in long-distance racing, in company with other Italian manufacturers, Laverda and Moto Guzzi.

Laverda got into big-bike production almost by accident. They were contracted to design and build a machine to an American company's specification, for sale in the US. They wanted to build a triple, but the Americans wanted a large displacement twin styled on the very popular Honda CB72/77 lightweights.

The result was the closely-finned 750 twin, looking just like an overgrown Honda 250; but the deal fell through and Laverda, having built the bikes, were left

with no alternative but to try to sell a bike they hadn't wanted to build in the first place. In relatively limited production, the 750 sold tremendously well in Europe, establishing a good reputation for Laverda as well as providing them with an income. Eventually they were able to build the bike they wanted, the big three-cylinder model – but not before they had produced racer versions of the twin for endurance events.

Although the Bultaco was still capable of winning at Barcelona, it was a 750 Honda which won the reborn Bol d'Or in '69. Entered by Japauto but accompanied by factory mechanics, this was one of three models specially prepared for the event.

Triumph's works triples were ideal long-distance racers but although they achieved plenty of results during the next couple of years the problems of the British industry brought the racing attempt to a standstill.

Honda continued to support their machines, using modifications made to the Daytona racers and letting the semi-official bikes be entered by the importers and dealers, like Japauto.

The 1969 Honda didn't vary a lot from the standard machine. It had twin disc front brakes and a two-leading shoe rear drum, de Carbon rear dampers and Dunlop K81 tyres. The joints on the frame were neater than the

The 77 RCB had lower top frame rails and an eccentric swing-arm spindle to give chain adjustment. Many features, including the FVQ dampers, long-life chain and Comstar wheels were used on production machines *(photo by Honda UK)*

production bikes, where brazing had replaced arc-welding, which suggested that the machines were hand-built. The carburetters were standard 26 mm Keihin and there were four open exhausts. There was presumably some increase in power though, because the gearing had been raised — the rear wheel sprocket had 38 teeth instead of the standard 45. The fuel tank held 28 litres and fuel consumption was reckoned to be about 33 mpg, (compared with around 22 mpg for the 76 RCB).

Entries continued along these semi-official lines, the motors being bored out to around 950 cc, and a UK machine, entered by Alf Briggs and ridden by Charlie Williams and John Williams, finished first at the Spa 24-hour race. Some help was forthcoming from Honda's Racing Service (RSC) but this was a small unit. Research at Honda tended to stagnate after the CB750; their engineers were tied up working on cars and on the new emission requirements.

By '73 there was a racing kit for the 750 which more or less brought the bikes up to Daytona specification but with a less violent camshaft. The frames were copied from the Daytona machines and were built in the UK from factory drawings. By this time Honda were claiming 90 bhp for the engine. Obviously they could see the

potential in long-distance events, the lack of any serious factory opposition (SIDEMM were entering Kawasakis on a similar basis) and the opportunity to show off roadster-based models without a Grand Prix budget.

RSC built a new 750 for 1975, based on the 500 four-cylinder roadster. This machine had plenty of performance but lacked reliability. It was raced only a few times and the project was aborted after their test rider, Sumiya, was killed that summer.

The same year Honda's vice-president Kawashima visited the Bol d'Or, which was going from strength to strength, and decided that this would be a good place to go racing — officially.

Back in Japan a Research and Development department had been set up, with a lot more scope than the old RSC. They produced the first RCB, based on the bottom half of the CB750 — and with the understanding that a roadster would eventually have to be developed from it. R

Factory support

& D were therefore working in the knowledge that they not only had to build a successful racer but that it would also have to be practical enough to pay for their keep.

The original motor displaced 941 cc, and this was increased to 997 and later 1000 cc. A gear primary drive replaced the chain used in the roadster, giving the RCB its characteristic whine and providing, incidentally, a convenient countershaft so that the alternator could be mounted above the gearbox, thus reducing engine width. The cylinder head was vastly different, with double overhead camshafts and four valves per cylinder. Various exhaust systems were tested to achieve the optimum blend of power, noise level and ground clearance. The chassis was conventional but used Lockheed brake calipers (which allow the pads to be changed without disturbing the installation) and de Carbon rear dampers.

There were many detail innovations around the bikes. They were using an experimental long-life chain which worked, but was noisy, when dry. The wheels were of a new construction, with alloy rims and hubs, located by five sets of 'spokes' which were riveted in place. In 1976 they used the steel-spoked Comstar wheels – as intended for the roadsters – in order to gain public confidence in the design.

The ignition system was self-powered, using a small

For the 1978 Bol d'Or, Honda Britain took over an entry from Guignabodet and serviced a machine built by the New Racing department. Ridden by Dave Emde and Harry Klinzmann, the NR RCB revved to 11,500 rpm and had an engine which was more violent than the regular endurance racers

(photo by John Robinson)

generator driven by one of the camshafts to supply the transistorised circuit. Lighting was provided by twin 55W Cibié units, with a conventional 12V battery carried in the seat tail.

The 32 mm Keihin carburetters had transparent float bowls, and on a compression ratio of 11·5:1, Honda were claiming 115 bhp at 9,000 rpm. It is interesting to note the emphasis put on rideability — constant velocity carbs would give less power than slide carburetters of the same size yet Honda had chosen to fit CV carbs because they give better economy, easier starting and more flexibility, making the engine easier for the rider to use. Still, power wasn't something they were short of; the RCBs had already kept up an average of 115 mph for the full 24-hours at Spa.

There was an official team of three of these bikes, later known as the 76s to distinguish them from later ver-sions, although no two were ever identical, being tailored to suit individual riders and having continual detail changes made. There were also back-up machines and a spare engine which was lent to Japauto. The British bike was ridden by Stan Woods and Jack Findlay at the Bol d'Or, Jack stepping in for regular rider Charlie Williams.

Honda France had Christian Léon, Jean-Claud Chemarin, René Guili, Hubert Rigal, Christian Huguet and Roger Ruiz, although Alex George deputised for the injured Léon at Le Mans. In this team they had some of the most experienced racers available, and it showed.

Charlie Williams demonstrates the RCB's ground clearance as he heels it into Druids on the way to a Brands Hatch victory

(photo by John Robinson)

Development continued. The 77 RCB was most easily identified by its new chassis. This had been lowered, following current endurance-racing trends, with the top frame rails going around the carburetters instead of over them, curving closely across the engine to a heavily triangulated steering head. The oil cooler was mounted in front of the steering head, with a duct in the fairing.

In fact, a lot more work had gone into the machines. The engine, now up to 997 cc and with a 10·5:1 compression ratio, was claimed to give 125 bhp. A lot of this increase was due to the modified Keihin carbs and the new exhaust system which also gave the remarkably low noise level of 106 dB, under the conditions set for the FIM noise test. The 77s had new front and rear suspension, the rear gas-oil dampers being built by Showa, a subsidiary of Honda Motor Co. Ltd. To speed up pit work, both wheels were QD, the rear wheel leaving both the sprocket and disc in place. The new chain was still under development – the intention being to make it last a whole 24-hour race with an acceptable noise level.

Perhaps the greatest achievement was also the least noticeable. They had reduced the machine's weight by some 20 kg. Carbon fibre was mixed with GRP for the fairing and seat, and many parts, including control levers, were either hollow or drilled. The conventional battery was discarded in favour of smaller, rechargeable, dry-cell batteries which were mounted under the seat. This wasn't a success and the 78 machines reverted to conventional batteries. Very light alloys were used around the bike and the wheels now had alloy instead of steel spokes.

The generators on the 77s gave trouble early in the season and were replaced by the lighting system from the 76.

Honda's RCBs dominated the endurance series in '76 and '77, although the dealer-sponsored Japauto team were leading the series at one stage. For 1978 a new RCB was produced, plus modified versions of the 77, uprated to 132 bhp. The first 78 carried its oil in the frame but this was raced only at Zandvoort and Barcelona. Honda once again won the *Coupe d'Endurance* and, by this time, R & D had pretty well fulfilled their brief. RCBs were virtually unbeatable in endurance racing – even keeping ahead of Yamaha racers in the short, 1,000 km event at Brands Hatch, although an OW31 had given them plenty of trouble at the '78 Bol d'Or. In addition to that there were the new roadsters, CB 900 FZ, the six-cylinder CBX and a new 750, which obviously owed a lot to the RCB design.

But before the new range of models was announced, many features first seen on the endurance racers had appeared in production. The roadsters benefited from the new chain, the excellent FVQ dampers and better lighting in the form of quartz-halogen H4 units fitted as standard.

Comstar wheels were used, first with steel and later with alloy spokes, and the exhaust design changed, allowing better engine performance with a high level of silencing. And, of course, the later bikes had the double overhead cam layout, with four valves per cylinder.

By '78 the endurance racers had reached their saturation point. There was nothing else left to win, and little that would significantly improve the RCB's overall performance. It was possible to get more power from the engine and Honda, planning a GP programme, had set up a New Racing department to develop four-strokes still further. NR modified an RCB for the '78 Bol d'Or, purely as an experiment. Ridden by Americans Klinzman and Emde, it was managed by the Honda Britain team and took over an entry by the French dealer, Guignabodet, with a claimed 140PS. The engine ran to 11,500 rpm, compared with 9,000 for the 76 and 9,500 for the 77 but the NR model proved less flexible than the standard RCBs. It was built to see how much power it would give, and for how long. The riders reported that it wasn't short on performance but that it wasn't so easy to ride. Obviously there was nothing at the Bol d'Or which the engineers couldn't simulate in Japan – except for the pressure on two newcomers (both to the circuit and to 24-hour racing) with a peaky engine in a heavy frame. The only problems with the bike were a split oil tank and two brake failures when disc run-out caused the pads to be pushed back into the cylinders.

The 78 RCB bore a closer resemblance to roadster practice, with the generator on one end of the crankshaft and the ignition unit on the other, the wider engine restricting ground clearance. On both this model and the late 77s, the engine could be moved around by using different engine plates, in order to alter the weight distribution. Throughout the season's racing the only mechanical problems were a cam failure at Le Mans and clutch trouble at Zandvoort.

After the success of the early RCBs, Honda Japan organised their racing in a thorough and comprehensive way. There had been several teams equipped with RCBs, plus others running modified 750s and even Gold Wings. France, Britain, Germany, Switzerland, Holland and Belgium were all represented with varying degrees of official support, plus teams like Japauto and Dholda who were given the use of RCB engines. To bring some order to this vast array, the Honda Endurance Racing Team was established. All the European subsidiaries contributed to this central fund and those who were taking part in the racing drew their expenses from it. Honda France, based in Paris, allocated workshop space to travelling race teams, while technicians from the factory travelled to the races and were on hand to help the teams.

Honda's involvement in endurance racing followed the classic pattern, starting with a casual interest and building up into full works effort. Their supreme position at the end of this four-year episode could have led to stagnation in the sport itself. If, for instance, Honda kept up a sustained effort, or were to make RCBs available as over-the-counter racers, it would, for most participants, be a lot easier to join them than to fight them. In that case, as with the Manx Norton and the 350 Yamaha, the spectators could look forward to a procession of similar bikes. And that would take away much of the appeal of long-distance racing because its attraction lies in the innovations and individualism, even the characters which the racing brings out. Honda's chosen alternative, to support F1 racing and develop GP machines, is by far the best for everyone.

Other factories supported endurance racing during the same period, but not on the same scale as Honda, and their machines were never a serious threat to the Japanese fours. However, Ducati made good use of the prototype class to develop their V-twins which were soon made available as touring bikes, or in the case of the 750 and 900 Desmo sports models, as very high performance

sportsters. BMW, Guzzi and Laverda entered their machines with enough success to enhance their reputations. These engines, along with the four-cylinder Japanese roadsters, were the mainstay of the private entry. Even when there was little hope of competing on even terms with the Japanese factory-prepared bikes, there were still plenty of competitors who got enough satisfaction merely out of taking part in the classic long-distance events. The spectators, too, recognise this aspect and the applause at the end of a wearying 24 hours is as enthusiastic for the runners-up as it is for the winners. The winners, however, have to face a second ordeal as they are mobbed and hoisted from their machines, eventually reaching the winner's rostrum

The Belgian Dholda team were given an RCB to replace their Honda specials and promptly scored a win at Spa with riders Luc and Buytaert staying ahead of the official French and British Hondas
(photo by Motorcycle Mechanics)

Factory support

without touching the ground.

One other factory has had as much impact as Honda, but they preferred to keep their distance, working on a semi-official basis, as Honda had in the early '70s. Kawasaki's 903 cc Z1 was the most powerful machine available when it was first announced, and more was available from the big, four-cylinder motor. Godier and Genoud, who had been racing an Egli-framed Honda, switched to the new Kawasaki powerplant in 1974, with immediate success, including a win at the Bol d'Or where three more Kawasakis followed them home.

SIDEMM, the French Kawasaki importer, had been

Laverda's liquid-cooled, V-6 prototype – neat, low and sleek, but it has a weight problem

(photo by John Robinson)

entering semi-official models from the 500 cc H1R two-stroke through to the new fours and were obviously encouraged by this new trend. Then they were approached by Pierre Doncque and Michel Lambert, two mechanical engineers, who wanted to build a cantilever frame for the 900. When SIDEMM found that Georges Godier was in favour of this idea, they gave their blessing and agreed to support the venture.

The now-famous frame was designed at a French university where a lot of trouble was taken to improve every aspect needed for endurance racing. As well as light weight, low frontal area and good handling, it needed comfort, ease of maintenance, rapid access and the necessary ground clearance.

Quite obviously, it worked. In 1975 the Godier-Genoud Kawasakis set new records – and standards – in endurance racing. At the Bol d'Or their machines finished

first, and third (Duhamel/Baldé) with another Kawasaki ridden by Estrosi/Husson in second place.

By the same time the next year, though, they were up against the first of the RCBs and were finding it tough going. The machines were only modified to simplify them, using, for example, gravity fuel feed instead of an electric pump. They also replaced the alternator and starter motor, despite the 10 kg weight penalty, because the Keihin Racing carburetter made the engines difficult to start. Honda were using CV carbs, but these were not available in the size Godier wanted.

Even without the bulky alternator, grounding had been a problem, so now the machine was lifted, by 35 mm at the adjustable rear suspension and by making up front fork stanchions 40 mm longer than the originals.

For the very fast Spa circuit they had used a wilder cam but kept the standard valve springs, which failed and let the adjusting shims fall out of place. The 'softer' Yoshimura cam was fitted for the Bol d'Or, and the valve seats were lowered to reduce the risk of the valves touching the pistons. Electronic ignition from a 700 Yamaha was used and Godier claimed 102 bhp at the rear wheel, at 9,000 rpm. More was possible but reliability suffered and, according to Godier, they had reached the limit — only the factory could make the necessary modifications to keep reliability in step with further development.

The shaft drive which failed during the race. The Laverda's swing-arm pivots on the gearbox and the engine/transmission block form a stressed part of the frame

(photo by John Robinson)

Factory support

SIDEMM had reached the point where they could no longer continue as the official team if Kawasaki Japan did not supply technical aid. This was not forthcoming and the SIDEMM machines slid further behind the Hondas. Kawasaki eventually set up a wholly-owned subsidiary to import their machines into France and the race effort ended. For '78 Godier prepared several Kawasakis for the Kool-sponsored team but they were basically standard machines and of five bikes at the Bol d'Or only one finished, and that was a Pipart Kawasaki.

Other factories began to take interest; Yamaha were building a V-4 endurance machine, a Yoshimura Suzuki GS1000 appeared at the '78 Bol d'Or and so did an interesting prototype from Laverda.

The Italian machine was a watercooled V-6, with

shaft drive and the engine stressed as part of the frame. It had transmission problems during practice, and retired from the race with a failed drive-shaft. Ing. Alfieri, who designed the 2·7 litre V-6 used in the Citroën-Maserati car, was responsible for the 1000 cc Laverda engine. The idea behind the project was to build a racer, then develop a roadster from it. Using the basic V-block could allow a range of V-twins, V-4 and V-6 engines, giving a range of 350 to 1200 cc.

The prototype engine had double overhead cams with four-valve heads and electronic ignition. Although the engine was quite long, the machine had a wheelbase of 57 inches, which is slightly shorter than the CBX. At 200 kg it was no lightweight, but this is similar to the weight of the first RCB machine.

Lucas and Kugelfischer fuel injection systems had been tried but were not consistent enough at high engine speeds and the prototype ran on Dell'Orto carburetters.

There is, it seems, ample material for the works-support cycle to begin again.

The V-6 is narrow where it counts, allowing the engine to be slung low down without sacrificing ground clearance *(photo by John Robinson)*

Chapter Eight
The specialists

The nature of long-distance racing sets it apart from other sports and it quite obviously has a special appeal to certain riders. They, in return, have developed their particular skills and have raised the state of the art to its present, highly-specialised form. In many cases it is simply because they like this kind of racing – some riders who could do well on the GP circuits have been forced to choose one type of racing or the other, because the crowded calendars do not permit both. For several years, one round of the endurance championship was held immediately before the TT and Charlie Williams, an ace in both fields, would practise in the Island, fly to the Continent for the endurance race and then fly back, just in time for the start of his TT ride. Literally just in time, because he would have to change into his leathers in the airport taxi and the travelling arrangements must have been as hectic as the racing.

In other cases, it has been the enthusiasm of endurance riders which kept the racing going during times when motorcycling was going through a depression. Then, when things got better, the same privateers would carry on with their humble budgets, against factory-built racers and the star riders employed to handle them.

Since the late '40s these specialists have emerged as a more important group. There was Gustave Lefèvre, a professional racer who, riding a 500 Norton, was unbeatable at the French Bol d'Or. The Belgian Jules Nies was a keen supporter of long-distance events and made his racing span a whole generation, co-riding with his son Charly during the '70s.

While the Spanish factories were working wonders with their lightweights, the big four-stroke twins remained the best bet for privateers. English riders like Peter Darvill contested most of the continental events and, like Nies, chose a BMW until the arrival of the Japanese fours. Despite the fact that there were no UK endurance races (or possibly because of it) more British riders began entering the continental events. Dave Degens, for example, found that his Dresda specials – originally Norton-Triumphs – were pretty well suited to this kind of racing, where he chalked up quite a few successes. The same machines, although based on production bikes, were not allowed to compete in British events. Other sponsors, such as Mead and Tomkinson,

took a liking to endurance racing and found that by concentrating on all the demands of a long-distance race, they could get results from quite modest machinery. Their single cylinder 500 BSA had an overall win at the Belgian 24-hour race at Zolder, numerous class wins, and always seemed to figure somewhere near the top of the overall placings.

By concentrating on preparing themselves and the machines specifically for long races, these specialists raised the level of competition until, when the big Japanese machines became available, it was already a big-time sport. Machine preparation and modification were moving at quite a pace – the Dresda bikes had special frames and, just before the introduction of disc brakes, an eight-leading-shoe drum brake. In an attempt to maintain powerful braking and not have to change the linings during the race, Degens was experimenting with alternate shoes fitted with 'racing' and 'roadster' lining material. Oddly enough it was the 'roadster' material which wore out first but the compound gave better wear characteristics than a brake fitted solely with hard, 'racing' linings and he claimed it would last a whole 24 hours at the twisty, Montjuich Park circuit.

Continental specialists, like Japauto and Offenstadt and later, d'Hollander, added their own particular brews, making use of the new Japanese power units in their own chassis and cycle parts. Ultimately Georges Godier showed how important these specials were, first with an Egli frame and later with the purpose-built, Kawasaki-powered devices. The success of these specialists no doubt prompted the factories to take more than a passing interest in endurance racing.

But all along, the privateers had been up against works entries with varying degrees of officialdom. Early on there had been the French Ydral lightweights, Austrian Puch machines, Ducatis from Italy and, of course, the Spanish two-strokes. BMW machines figure all the way through, often with some factory backing and later, full prototypes which anticipated the following 900 and 980 cc roadsters.

Triumph, Moto Guzzi and Laverda all used endurance races to show off and develop their big roadster-based machines, while semi-official Hondas and Kawasakis gradually appeared, with race-tuned versions of their roadster engines. The climax came with Honda's own purpose-built racers, the RCBs which dominated endurance events.

At their best, the works machines overshadowed private entries, but they were still there, as enthusiastic as ever and not letting the rather biased competition deter their efforts. And in these efforts many unusual, not to say unlikely, machines appeared. The Swiss Honda importer used two Gold Wings in highly specialised frames – with some success, although a similar venture in the UK proved that the Honda's three-bearing crank-

shaft restricted its reliability in racing trim.

Another Honda dealer, the Belgian d'Hollander, tried a similar approach to that of Japauto, using 750-based machines in special chassis. The Dholda bikes were framed with a maze of triangulations and the rear wheel was carried on a subframe which pivoted on two swinging forks. A similar design had been tried on GP bikes, where it had proved to be too heavy – but on the big endurance racers it was competitive, especially as their problem at the time was chain wear. The unusual suspension on the Dholda reduced the fluctuations in chain tension as the wheel went up and down. But, like the Swiss effort, the design was outdated by developments on the official RCBs, and eventually both teams reverted to the new racers.

There were many dealer entries from the Continent who specialised in endurance racing, usually using Kawasaki or Honda engines with similar degrees of tuning, but fitted into their own chassis. Concerns like Pipart, National Moto, Durano, Motoplast, Van der Waal and Martin used Kawasakis; Motorrad Meyer, Freyters, Japauto and d'Hollander used Hondas; machines such as the Ducatis and Laverdas were campaigned by Val d'Oise, SNCM, and so on.

British interest grew, as well, helped more recently

Opposite **The pit straight at Spa and the start of the 1977 24-hour race**
(photo by Honda UK)
Below **The Dresda Triumph used for the 1970 Barcelona race – the beginning of the era when the specialists started to make significant changes**
(photo by Motorcycle Mechanics)

The specialists

by the successful launch of F1 racing which supplied a formula similar to that of the existing prototypes. Gus Kuhn Motors sponsored first a BMW and then a GS Suzuki with riders like Potter, Sharpe, Cowie, Nichols and Goldsmith. Big Kawasakis appeared in the hands of Trimby, Crosby, Hatton, Wells and Osborne. Honda-based machines were ridden by Winfield, Camier, Copland and Lee. Apart from the earlier Mead and Tomkinson entries and the Dresda machines, the most successful British entry has probably been the Albion Motors Kawasaki, ridden by John Cowie and Bernie Toleman. Cowie used a similar machine to win the 1978 British Formula One Championship, and his endurance racer was often in the first half-dozen finishers, regularly getting among the works-entered bikes. The Cowie/Toleman Kawasaki had its best result in a non-championship race, when it won the 1,000 km event at Mettet. At the 24 heures du Mans, another non-championship race, they finished third, with Gary Green

Another view of the 1970 Dresda Triumph with its fuel tank removed

(photo by Motorcycle Mechanics)

and Marc Fontan sharing a Japauto in 6th place.

In the FIM series, Cowie and Toleman scored a 4th at Spa, and when injuries put John Cowie out of action, Toleman shared the bike with Steve Eldridge to come 12th at the Bol d'Or and, with co-rider Graeme Crosby, to finish 7th at the Brands Hatch 1,000 km race. Richard Peckett, of the Peckett and McNab partnership, rode the team's other machine with Tony Holland to finish 6th in this race, behind Gary Green and Bernard Murray on a Honda Britain RCB.

The P & M-framed Kawasaki, sponsored by Albion Street Motors, remained remarkably competitive, keeping amongst the works bikes and usually being more than a match for the continental privateers.

Apart from the official Honda entries, the only other British rider to figure in the results lists was Pete Davies, who shared a 500 Laverda with Agusto Brettoni and

The Dresda's front wheel — K81 tyre and a self-balancing linkage to operate the four leading-shoe drum brake. A similar backplate is fitted on the far side, giving eight leading shoes

(photo by Motorcycle Mechanics)

finished 9th at Barcelona.

Despite its increasingly popularity, endurance racing is no small undertaking for a privateer or even a dealer-sponsored team. It represents a large investment and commitment, not only in keeping the machinery competitive, but also in the essential back-up facilities. For the rider there is no club-level 'training' ground – there have been 1,000 km production races, but these offer little likelihood of attracting a sponsor. The only level of endurance racing is international and those who decide to jump in soon find that the deep end is the only end.

The races are Internationals, often on an invitation basis, held under general FIM rules, but each with their own detail regulations. The Bol d'Or for example. caters for sports and prototype machines of 251–1200 cc, while the Belgian 24-hour race is for sports or production machines of 175–1000 cc and prototypes from 241–1000 cc. Two riders must be used, although three may be nominated in the entry, and each rider may not ride for more than three hours at a time. After this he must have a rest of at least one hour, and, if his co-rider is injured or can no longer ride, he can continue alone on

this basis as long as he doesn't exceed two-thirds of the race time. In events where the stints are around 1 hour to 1 hr 20 min before refuelling, the riders often do a double stint during the night – coming in for fuel and taking the bike out again – in order to give the longest rest break to their partners.

The entry free and insurance cover for the '78 Bol d'Or was 400F (about £50). For the winner there was 50,000F, going down to 1,200F for 12th place. From 13th onwards all teams which qualified – that is, completed 75 per cent of the winner's distance – received

Opposite **Hub centre steering sets off Mead and Tomkinson's 1976 racer which was powered by a three-cylinder Laverda**
(photo by Motorcycle Mechanics)
Below **The later variants used on Kawasaki engine with the fuel tank fixed below the motor. Note the repositioned caliper on the front brake, moved because wheel bearing play caused run-out at the disc which pushed the pads away from the disc surface** *(photo by John Robinson)*

The specialists

1,000F. A similar system was operated in Belgium; the prizes from 1st down to 12th ranged from 14,000FB to 5,500FB and all qualifiers received 5,000FB. Any teams who completed the 24 hours but did not qualify were given 3,500FB, which was the same as their entry fee. Occasionally, organisers pay start money and there are other incentive variations such as the supply of petrol at reduced prices.

During scrutineering, the frame, crankcase and gearbox case are marked and these components may not be changed, although any other parts can be replaced and repairs can be made during the race. Parts normally

A BMW undergoes a transmission overhaul in the paddock at Spa

(photo by Motorcycle Mechanics)

covered by scrutineering, such as oil drain plugs which must be locked, obviously have to be refitted to the same standards if they are disturbed and if a fresh exhaust system is to be used it must bear a mark indicating that it has been passed during scrutineering.

Lighting obviously has to be fitted for the 24-hour races and the regulations usually ask for standards similar to road practice for lenses and reflectors. The Bol d'Or regulations demand a rear, red reflecting plate of 225 cm² and two tail-lights (or two bulbs with independent circuits housed inside one lamp unit). Lights have to be used whenever a signal is displayed on the pit straight. At some of the shorter events the regulations are not quite so clear-cut – at one Italian race, where the track was floodlit, the organisers said that lighting wasn't needed. Then, after the race had started, someone decided that it was – and the leading teams had to fit makeshift lights

rapidly in order to avoid possible disqualification at the end.

The Le Mans type start has become traditional for the major events, the machines being lined up at the trackside according to their performance in practice and the riders sprinting across the track to start them up. Anyone making a false start has a ten-minute penalty awaiting them and only the rider is allowed to start the bike. The rules governing pit stops are devised to make things as safe as possible and the layout of the pit road obviously influences this. Often a klaxon is sounded each time a machine pulls off the circuit to come into the pits and a marshal is positioned to control traffic pulling away from the pits on to the main circuit.

Regulations for the Bol d'Or imposed a speed limit of 80 km/h along the decelerating lanes and pit road, and once the bike has stopped in the pits its engine has to be cut. Any oil change or machine cleaning has to be carried out over a drip tray and the team managers are responsible for keeping their pit bay cleaned. Marshals at each pit report on the work being carried out and check that safety regulations are enforced. Refuelling is either by can or by a derrick-mounted dump tank, which has to be covered, contain no more than 40 litres and have its vents pointing downwards. The machines' fuel tanks are restricted to 24 litres and the team is not allowed to store more than a total of 80 litres. Although it has not been unknown for teams to have a separate seat/tank unit tailored to suit each rider, refuelling by changing the tank

Rolling chassis of an RCB ... the easiest way to keep a complete stock of spare parts

(photo by John Robinson)

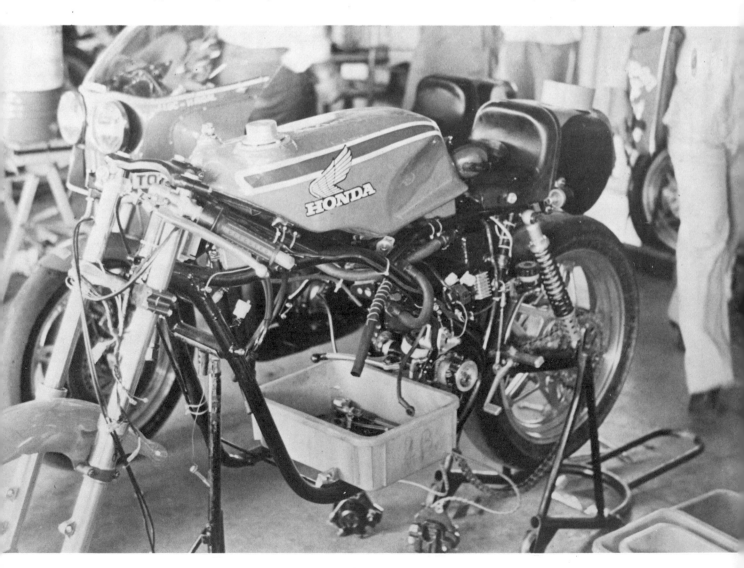

The specialists

is forbidden. A team is allowed two mechanics who are not to work outside their pit area or to work on bikes belonging to other teams, and only two people are allowed to work on a bike at the same time. The rider, as long as he remains seated on the machine is excluded from this.

On leaving the pit it is usually easier for the teams to push-start the bikes, even though they are fitted with kick-starts or starter motors. Slave batteries are not allowed in the refuelling area and the rules also state that only one person may push the bike – and, once the last pit has been reached, the rider must continue on his own,

The fast, left-right switch, looking down from the pits at Spa

(photo by Motorcycle Mechanics)

which was bad news for the people already in the last pit. For riders who strike trouble on the circuit, the only way to stay in the race is to push the bike along the right hand kerb or in the safety lane – cutting corners or accepting outside help means disqualification. Of course, on some circuits, like the long road circuit at Spa, such rules are easier to write than to enforce. There are many stories about riders who were pushing in with an empty tank, out in the total darkness of the Ardennes, when they stumbled across a container of fuel at the side of the road.

On this very long circuit, the race finishes when the first bike crosses the line after 24 hours and there is often a weary figure sitting on a broken machine at the beginning of the downhill finish straight. Having pushed to this point where he can coast to the finish line, all he has to do is hope that he judges the time correctly and coasts

down *after* the race has been declared finished. At other races, like the Bol d'Or, the race ends when the leading machine crosses the line after the 24 hours are up. Everyone else must complete their lap within six minutes for it to be counted and those who have covered at least 75 per cent of the winner's distance are classified in the results.

During the course of such long races it is easy to break some of the many rules, either accidentally or as the only way to keep the machine running. The penalty is an official warning, on the grounds that it could happen to anyone once or twice – but if it happens three times the offenders are deemed to be pushing their luck and get disqualified.

The teams will have a day, possibly two days, of practice in order to get their machines set up, familiarise themselves with the track and work out a routine for their

pit stops and rider changes. The longer the race, the more important it is for them to be able to judge these stops, calculate fuel consumption, tyre wear and all the little detail jobs that could prove crucial to the race. Some of the practice sessions will be in the dark if the race itself runs through the night and there will officially timed sessions which dictate the riders' position on the start grid. This is where the teams can weigh up the opposition and where the favourites can do their best to demoralise their competitors.

The Honda France team made a point of going hard in practice – often getting the big RCB around as quickly

Below and following two pages **Variations in lighting ... Hella ... Cibie ... SEV Marchal ... and Bosch** *(photos by Motorcycle Mechanics)*

The specialists

as machines like the Suzuki RG500s had lapped in Grand Prix races. They would push themselves this hard even though it meant taking chances, like risking slick tyres on a circuit which still had damp patches. For all the competitors, practice was vital to rehearse pit stops and, if everything went smoothly with the machine, to work out fuel consumption and so on.

Naturally the teams would be well-rehearsed with their own machines and pit equipment. But the pits and the approach road into the pits vary from circuit to circuit, often dictating changes in the layout of the equipment and the procedure for getting the bike in, refuelling and away again as quickly and smoothly as possible. The

The Offenstadt 350 Yamaha, with trailing link front forks *(photo by Motorcycle Mechanics)*

tools, fuel, oil, tyres and engine spares need to be stored in the pit in such a way that the crew can find any given item immediately; the timekeepers need to be perched up on a comfortable seat where they can have a clear view of the machines on the track and some system of pit signalling has to be devised. This, and the team's calculations on fuel consumption, are just as essential as the riders' ability to go quickly. Ideally, they would hope to bring the bike in for refuelling with just a couple of litres in the tank — to bring it in earlier would be a waste, to leave it later would be to risk running the tank dry. A change in the race conditions, such as rain, would obviously affect the fuel consumption and the range given by one tankful.

For the riders, the most important thing is to establish a rhythm for riding around the circuit, to strike a balance between going fast and taking unnecessary

chances. If a rider can lap consistently, taking the same line, braking and changing gear in the same places each time, it is easier to pace himself for the long stints and far less tiring than if he plays it by ear. Such a rhythm is also helpful when night falls and the track and trackside markers take on an entirely new perspective. Things which are clearly visible in daylight, even dominating the view, can disappear altogether, being replaced by totally different landmarks picked out by the machine's headlamps. If the rider relied on this new view, he would have to learn the circuit all over again and would lap more slowly in the dark. By getting into a known rhythm, it's easier to keep up the pace, particularly on corners which suddenly become blind when trackside features disappear in the dark, leaving no clue as to which way the road goes. Then the rider has to reassure himself that he has got the right rhythm. He brakes hard, with shrinking

visibility as the forks compress and the light beam contracts back up the road. He knows – hopes – that when he has changed down two gears it will be time to lay the bike hard over and then, when he is pretty well committed, the light will sweep round in a crazy, tipped-up arc and he will be able to see the track again.

It isn't surprising, as the surrounding features merge into a solid darkness, that the crisp exhaust notes change into stuttering, on-off crackles as the riders feed the machine into bends. It is surprising that many of them still lap within a second or two of their daylight speeds.

The 76 Japauto Honda with elaborately styled glass fibre. The Paris-based firm were one of the first to use big-bore four-cylinder engines

(photo by Motorcycle Mechanics)

The first job of the pit crew is to keep a check on the bike's progress – apart from needing to know where they are in the race, it also gives advance warning of any trouble if the bike doesn't come through on schedule, and they have to know when to expect the bike in order to put out their pit signals. So the timekeepers will be checking off each lap, as well as keeping an eye on the race leaders and on their nearest competitors. At some circuits it is essential to make sure the signals go out to the right rider. The pit straight at Spa is downhill, with a sweeping right-hand curve in it and a fast, left-right switch at the bottom of the hill. The pits are on the rider's right; he comes out of the slow la Source hairpin, drifting out to the left as he puts on full power and, on the approach to the pits, throws the bike over hard to the right. As he passes the first pit stands the bike will be well banked over, up close to the Armco and still accelerating hard. The rider will be pulling it back, trying to keep it over to the right and setting it up for the next bend, with its violent change of road camber.

For the teams in the centre of the pits, all that can be seen is the headlamp beam sweeping around the hairpin, climbing up across the trees and back to the track. Then there will be a blaze of lights as the bike appears, already banked over and coming straight towards them, flashing past at over 100 mph. They have no more than a couple of seconds to decide whether it is their machine and to hold out the signal board.

Normally the pit signals will merely tell the rider what his last lap time was, whether he is gaining or losing ground, or simply to come in to the pits. Apart from the occasional, cryptic humour, there is nothing more the rider needs to know, except that there is still someone there cheering him on and that they haven't all given up and gone home. Few team managers will try to control a rider; out on the circuit they let him make the decisions. Occasionally they might urge him on but as a psychological boost rather than a 'go faster' instruction. Possibly the biggest value of the pit signals is simply to keep up the rider's morale and to keep the pit crew awake! On the other hand the team manager might slow the bike down,

Opposite top **Dave Degens, once a constructor of endurance-winning machines came back to the '76 Bol d'Or to ride the big Japauto with Bernard Sailler**
(photo by Motorcycle Mechanics)
Opposite bottom **Sleek lines of the graceful Moto Guzzi but the Italian V-twins were outgunned by the big Japanese fours**
(photo by Rod Sloane)
Below **The highly professional Pipart team managed to keep their Kawasakis up with the works Hondas**
(photo by Motorcycle Mechanics)

if he is aware of some problem such as tyres overheating or if they are keeping the bike circulating with a makeshift repair while something more permanent is being rigged up in the pit.

Signals from the rider are usually restricted to an acknowledging wave or nod. Riders often go past pointing down at something on the machine; most teams regard this as an indication that something is wrong and get ready for an unscheduled stop, but there is little to be gained from trying to read something into the rider's signal or trying to guess what is wrong. There is more to be learned from the lap times, judging whether the rider

Opposite top **Once the dominant force in long-distance racing, the Kawasakis were still the only serious threat to the works Hondas and came in many guises, one of which was the National Motos prototypes**
Opposite bottom **The Belgian specialists D'Hollander had to let their unorthodox special play second string to the RCB** *(photos by John Robinson)*
Below **Stalwarts of the endurance world, the beautifully turned-out Val d'Oise Ducati** *(photo by Rod Sloane)*

is easing off, battling with some persistent trouble, or whether he simply made a mistake and lost a few seconds.

Watching the machine, listening to it and making a note of what is going on around the other teams can help to prepare the crew for possible problems. If other teams are having misfire problems or trouble with tyres, it suggests a more general fault rather than something peculiar to one machine. The crew would at least be prepared for similar trouble, refuelling through a filter mesh, for example, or being prepared to swap the whole bank of carburetters. Anticipating trouble in this way and being prepared for it is where a good team manager earns his keep.

Just as the riders and their crews needs to get into a regular rhythm, most of the longer races follow a pattern. In 24-hour events there is usually a 3 pm or 4 pm start and the riders will go hard during the first hour or two, trying to get among the leaders and to establish a rhythm which will keep them near the front. Equally, riders who have got a good start will be trying to break away from the pack and build up a good lead — often the racing is as close as in a short circuit race.

During this first hour there will be more than an

average number of pit stops. If a mechanical part is going to fail, it will usually do so quite quickly and a few bikes will retire very early in the race with holed pistons and similar damage. Other teams will be discovering faults in their preparation and there will be the odd machine doing a few laps and then returning to its pit while the source of the trouble is traced and fixed.

There might be six hours of racing before it gets dark and after the initial bout of problems, things tend to settle down. The field strings out, with six or a dozen bikes all keeping first place in their sights. The riders settle down into their own pace and things calm down, giving the pit crews a chance to relax. Darkness brings the next batch of trouble and between 10 pm and midnight there will be more unscheduled stops, with lighting failures and crashes as riders make mistakes in the changing conditions.

Through the early hours of the morning things settle down again as the riders readjust, machines coming in for routine tyre and brake changes. The biggest problem is rain, the riders not noticing the first light drops until the track is damp, and then finding it difficult to slow down enough to cope with the conditions. Things start to pick up from dawn onwards, although some machines will be

showing signs of wear and tear and the circuit is noticeably quieter, the exhausts losing their crisp, raucous edge. Towards midday the pace quickens up as riders see the opportunity to catch up a few more places in traffic which has been thinned down by retirements. There will be the odd bike pressing on slowly, trying to last until the finish. For some reason this always seems to be a good time for punctures and for things like electrical failures and quite often trouble like this causes dramatic changes on the leaderboard.

For the last few hours most riders will be concentrating on keeping in touch with the bike in front, catching and passing it if possible, to move up one place. But there will still be a few machines racing hard, making up lost time or fighting to work their way up the leaderboard.

Opposite **A few serious attempts to build long-distance machines out of short-distance racers resulted in bikes which were long on performance but short on endurance. This 750 Yamaha is equipped with two-way radio**
Below **More Suzuki power, prepared by the British Gus Kuhn team** *(photos by John Robinson)*

The specialists

Towards the end, the overall winner will probably have a safe enough lead and only a crash or mechanical failure would make any big change. The crowds build up and slowly press towards the finishing straight in an overwhelming tide which, minutes before the end, breaks through the barriers and police cordons to swamp the track, leaving a narrow passage for the finishing bikes to filter through. Being hoisted bodily from the machine and passed shoulder-high up to the rostrum has convinced many winners that there's a lot to be said for finishing second!

Despite the pace, the obvious physical and mental effort of long-distance racing, the teams are not just competing against one another. They are all up against a

Bimota frame, Suzuki engine. A new generation of roadsters could supply the necessary hardware for further development *(photo by Motorcycle Mechanics)*

natural law that if something can go wrong, it *will* go wrong. It leads to highly competitive racing on the track, but a friendly, co-operative atmosphere within the paddock and pits. At the Brands Hatch 1,000 km event, Honda Britain, who were closer to their Chiswick base than they'd been all season, discovered that their metal dump-tank, as required in the Brands regulations, was in fact a slow-filler. The French Pipart team, rivals who ran Kawasakis, didn't hesitate to lend them their spare quick-filler.

Some years ago, the *Motorcycle Mechanics* 500 Suzuki had a habit of developing hairline cracks in its front hub. During practice at the Bol d'Or, all the spare wheels were found to be cracked and a 'phone-call to the nearest distributor failed to produce any replacements. The race organisers broadcasted an appeal for help and within minutes three spectators turned up in the paddock, carrying the wheels they had removed (presumably!) from their own roadsters. Their generosity

was rewarded in an ironic way — on examining the wheels, all three proved to have worse cracks than those on the racer ...

Incidents like these spontaneous gestures are not unusual, overcoming red tape and language barriers alike — most of the time. The French rider Berger shared a 500 BSA with Nigel Rollason at another Bol d'Or event, backed up by an all-English pit crew. The Frenchman arrived hastily in the pits, saying that he was having trouble with the clutch ('embrayage'). The mechanics promptly and rapidly stripped out the ignition ('allumage') before he could stop them.

Endurance racing is taken seriously, particularly by the French. What it means to them was summed up by an experience in '78. The weekend of the Finnish GP, which could have been crucial in the battle between Kenny Roberts and Barry Sheene for the 500 cc World Championship, I was in central France and keen to find out the result of this race. I bought a regional paper, Midi

Libre. On the sports page there was a longish piece about a local race at Nîmes and a paragraph saying that Nieto had won the Finnish 125 GP (proving they had a correspondent or agency reports from the GP) and another, longer piece describing the first Japanese endurance race. In the Suzuka 8-hours, Americans Wes Cooley and Mike Baldwin won on a Suzuki GS1000. It happened in front of a 70,000 crowd and the works RCB of Léon and Chemarin had gone out with mechanical trouble. The British RCB had gone out on the first lap, when Stan Woods crashed on spilt oil.

A similar Suzuki made its European début later that year at the event which must epitomise endurance racing, the Bol d'Or ...

And from America, the Yoshimura Suzuki, raced at the '78 Bol d'Or, with Pops Yoshimura in the background *(photo by Rod Sloane)*

Chapter Nine
The Bol d'Or

The Bol d'Or 24-hour race is a story in its own right. Dating back to 1922, this French classic must be the oldest surviving day-and-night event in motorcycle racing. It dominates the endurance calendar, carrying the richest prizes with the prestige and sheer spectacle worthy of a World Championship event.

But it too has had its ups and downs, changing with the periodic booms and slumps in motorcycling. Although it has always been a 24-hour race, its format and regulations have changed to follow motorcycling trends. At the end of the '50s it was even suspended through lack of support, to be resurrected nine years later when the popularity of bikes soared upwards once more.

Its beginning coincided with a new phase in motorcycle racing. The first race was run on May 27, 1922 over a road circuit passing Livry-Gargan and Vaujours, within a few miles of the Porte de Pantin on the outskirts of Paris. Up to this time, racing was held either on short oval circuits or over point-to-point, cross-country routes which travelled from town to town on public roads. The Isle of Man TT races came into this category because, although the route formed a circuit, it was long and tortuous enough to be distinguished from any kind of 'circuit' racing.

This was the era when road racing was just that, except that 'road' didn't necessarily imply a smooth, metalled surface. The idea of a purpose-built race track, other than the short ovals or banked, wooden-board tracks, hadn't germinated. Machines either went from A to B or they chased one another round in small circles. The new Bol d'Or, while held on public roads, also formed a short circuit.

When the magazine *Moto Revue*, who still sponsor the race, announced the first event, their headlines proclaimed non-stop racing for 50 hours. For there was to be a 24-hour race for motorcycles on May 27–28, followed by a similar event for up-to-1100 cc cyclecars and up-to-1000 cc sidecars going through to May 29. The winner, in each category, would be the machine which covered the greatest distance inside 24 hours and, to qualify, each entrant had to travel at least 90 km within the first three hours. After that, a stop of up to four hours was permitted — and would probably be necessary because each motorcycle had only one rider.

There were three categories for bikes, 250, 350 and 500 cc, and the first four riders in each class were to receive medals.

This race was held one year before the 24-hour car race run on the road circuit at Le Mans, so it was bikes which sparked off the French passion for long-distance racing. The Vaujours circuit was, as *Moto Revue's* reporter found, a more or less convenient tram ride from his office, plus a lengthy walk:

'The circuit wasn't too bad but was, alas, poorly placed for the spectator who only had legs! The Gargan-Opéra tram is capricious, it drops slowly towards the South and only makes up its mind, after a good half-hour, to turn East, in the correct direction.'

Luckily, though, the intrepid reporter got his story, which was that a 500 cc Motosacoche travelled 1,245·628 km to lead home 14 finishers out of 17 starters. In the following race, only four of the cyclecars bettered this distance.

The race had taken off — to such an extent that 74 entries swamped the 1923 event. This time, on a road circuit at St. Germain, the sidecars lined up with the solos leaving the cyclecars to battle it out for themselves on the second and third days. The increased entry also called for further sub-divisions in the solo classes. There were *vélomoteurs* (motorised cycles) of 75, 100 and 125 cc, motorcycles of 250, 350 and 500 cc and the sidecars of 350, 600 and 1000 cc. A points system of scoring was devised, allowing the classes to start separately.

This kind of complication, with nine class winners, was to confuse the organisers, spectators and time-keepers throughout the history of this type of event. The 500 cc solo class dominated the race, a Sunbeam winning in 1924 covering a record 1,535 km.

More than 100 entries for the following year's race confirmed the popularity of the event and people were waking up to the publicity value of winning. Also, a machine which was easily ridden in the race obviously offered the same virtues for normal road use. *Moto Revue* noted, in 1926, that the winning 500 Sunbeam was the only machine to be fitted with an automatic ignition advance which allowed the rider to 'lap with surprising consistency and without any labour'.

For 1927 the race moved temporarily to a road circuit which formed the three sides of a triangle, just outside Fontainebleau. By now it had been narrowed down to seven classes — 125, 175, 250, 350 and 500 solos, plus 350 and 600 sidecars. But the organisers were still offering three solid days of racing, and there were seven classes of cars as well.

The attitude toward this kind of racing was that it was the *rider* who won — and on his part it certainly was a

Opposite **The Frutschi/Fougeray Godier-Kawasaki**
(photo by Motorcycle Mechanics)

The Bol d'Or

feat of endurance. Out of 67 starters in 1929 there were 51 finishers, many riders dropping out from fatigue.

In the columns of *Moto Revue*, a correspondent suggested a change in the rules to allow co-riders to take part — 'even though it goes against the due purpose of the event. Although it is a man's performance which is sought, one cannot demand this physical effort in a mechanical sport.'

The writer had a point which wasn't to be officially recognised until 25 years later. In fact the argument wasn't about safety but simply to ensure that the bike pressed on as long and as hard as possible. The failure

rate wasn't particularly high and the crashes involved collisions or incidents such as a rider stopping to change a spark plug and being hit by another machine as he worked at the side of the road.

Up to this point the bikes were strictly standard production machines but modifications gradually crept in. Open exhausts were used, other changes being aimed mainly at rider comfort, such as extra padding on the seat and tank, modified control levers, rocking-pedal gearshifts, bigger fuel and oil tanks and new lighting.

It was becoming an important event. By 1930 some 50,000 spectators were attracted to the race and this in turn prompted manufacturers to set up displays where their goods could be seen, as well as advertising successes in the race itself. It was being referred to as the Derby of motorcycling and the pressure on the racers can be judged from an analysis of the 1930 results. Out of 11

Formation racing 1. The Godier-Genoud Kawasakis line up along the pit straight

(photo by Motorcycle Mechanics)

sidecar entrants there were 6 retirements. The solos fared slightly better – from 44 entries, 25 reached the finishing line.

Of those who retired, 7 did so from mechanical failure, 5 from fatigue, 2 from crashes, 4 for unspecified reasons and 1 unfortunate ran out of fuel. The critics were obviously right in saying that rider fatigue was an important issue.

The event was also becoming an important showground for manufacturers and firms dealing in accessories, although 'show' was perhaps the operative word if an incident reported in 1931 is anything to go by. A stand had been set up at the trackside by a firm making shock absorbers and steering dampers. It happened that 'a rider broke his steering damper. He bounced up to the said stand. No one replied to his calls. He looked ... there was a stand right enough but it was hopelessly empty.'

By 1932 more detail modifications were appearing on the machines. Additional fuel tanks appeared on the sidecar outfits, while a 1000 cc JAP Bernadet also featured a guard over the carburetter intake to prevent the rider's clothing being sucked in. A Jonghi was fitted with an extra large fuel tank and a remote gearshift, using a parallelogram linkage and a rocking pedal so that the rider only had to press downwards with his heel or toe in order to change up or down through the gearbox. The 500 Motobécane used a four-valve cylinder head while more detail innovations appeared on other machines such as a small lamp to illuminate the manual oil pump control.

Formation racing 2. The works Hondas choose line abreast *(photo by Motorcycle Mechanics)*

The Bol d'Or

The following year *Moto Revue* noted that with 110 entries (including the cars), 48 hours of racing and average speeds of 80 km/h, there was not one accident resulting in serious injury. That was worthy of note then – and now. Considering the distance, time and speed involved, endurance racing probably has the best safety record of all motor racing.

A lack of development on the Continent was suggested by comments on a 6 year-old 175 cc Alcyon which, with hairpin valve springs and a compression ratio of 'only 6·3:1', was noted for its turn of speed. And by the appearance of a 350 Velocette which had a specially constructed 6-litre oil tank.

The Honda Suisse Gold Wing, ridden by Burki/Mooser
(photo by Motorcycle Mechanics)

1934 was the first time that anyone had exceeded 2,000 km during the race – and it was Willing's 350 Velo which recorded 2,031 km, beating all the 500s. Other items of interest (for future reference, perhaps) were a Peugeot 515 which had a left-foot gearshift conversion and a Royal Enfield combination with the passenger's grab rail welded to the exhaust pipe. It is not clear whether this was intended to cure cold hands or to keep the passenger awake!

The 350s were out in force, winning the 1935 race as well; this time it was Bourra riding a Norton. One of the sidecars – a Prester-Jonghi Bernadet – anticipated the Guzzis and RCBs of the '70s by using hydraulically operated brakes which were linked front and rear. Many sports models of the mid-30s were similar to their racing versions and it cannot have been easy to draw the line between what was considered standard production and

what was a racer. Whatever the theory, a 500 racing JAP, with virtually no cylinder head finning and a home-made oil cooler, was entered, but it didn't stop the 350s making it five in a row.

This in turn prompted one of *Moto Revue's* correspondents to analyse the situation. 350s had won for five years running and the only logical reason offered was that they were lighter and more manageable. The writer disagreed, saying that it was sheer force of numbers. In 1931 there had been plenty of rapid 350s with good riders, while no one of any consequence had chosen a 500. The same thing happened in 1932, with only a 500 Rudge in with a chance and that had a brake failure. 1933 saw three 500 riders capable of winning — one forgot to re-oil and blew his motor, another broke two fuel tanks. In '34 and '35 there were plenty of 500s but they all dropped out. The writer ended by prophesy-ing a win for the 500s.

He was right. The 1936 Bol d'Or went to the Gillet-Herstal 500 with a record distance of 2,068 km. (But a 350 Velo came second). The winning bike had front suspension made from rubber links — not unlike the Hagon fork used for grass track racing — and duralumin hubs. More serious modifications were also creeping in. One Motobécane had special alloy casings, different cams and carburetter.

In 1937 the event moved to Montlhéry, but amid bickering amongst the organising clubs the amateur riders boycotted the race. From an entry of close to 50, only 17 machines made the start line (or 18 if you count

Dave Croxford on the RCB-powered Japauto
(photo by Motorcycle Mechanics)

one who had completed 4 laps after nine hours). More reorganisation obviously took place, because the following year there were classes for amateur and professional riders as well as the solo and sidecar machine categories. The results, from 29 amateur riders and 29 professionals, hint that all was still not well. A 1000 cc sidecar came in first, followed by a 250 solo and a 600 sidecar. The first 500 was eighth. But arguments on a more international level overshadowed the Bol d'Or problems.

The race was reinstated in 1947 at St. Germain and won by Gustave Lefèvre on a plunger-frame 500 Norton. While the usual race modifications consisted of a large

roll of foam to cushion the rider, a Triumph twin appeared, fitted with a huge Harley-Davidson saddle ...

The 1948 race was boycotted by the professional riders, Lefèvre saying he'd been treated badly in '47. But he was back again for '49, still on a 500 Norton complete with an extra spotlamp mounted on a fork leg. Most riders still used standard handlebars or short, straight bars but one bike, a Sartum, had some chopped and welded bars which curved downwards not unlike 'Ace' bars.

Two more classes were added for 1950, allowing machines of 50 and 75 cc to compete and, fore-runner of a downhill slide, the first scooter (an AGF) was entered. Small bike popularity was emphasised when a 250 Guzzi won the 1952 race at an average 97 km/h, although the smallest class was lifted back to 125 cc. In post-war Europe the motorcycle industry was in the doldrums. The

Urgency in the Honda pit; oil on the rear tyre was making life interesting for Tony Rutter and Phil Read
(photo by Rod Sloane)

only demand was for cheap, utilitarian transport and big machines slowly disappeared, taking the factories with them. Later, as people became more affluent, there would be no large machines to buy. Even in the late '60s the sight of an ordinary BSA or Triumph twin would draw a crowd in France. In the '50s, the situation stifled races like the Bol d'Or and the essential support from industry and the public slowly dwindled away.

It was a time for the innovator, though. In 1952 a Monet-Goyon, powered by a 250 Villiers, ran with a two-plug head and external transfer ports. Its full-width front hub was able to accept a brake-plate on either side, although only one was used, fitted with twin cams. Thus a four-leading-shoe brake was a possibility. The 175 DS Malterre went even further, featuring a triangulated swinging arm which operated a linkage below the engine to compress a suspension unit – even the Godier-Genoud frame design wasn't entirely new!

The points about rider fatigue and safety were again being made – the rules still allowed only one rider per machine – and *Moto Revue* gave prominence to a highly critical letter which also pointed out that the Le Mans 24-hour car race permitted two drivers. Nothing happened until the following year, 1953, when the Bol d'Or was 25 years old. The gradual decline of the race was becoming evident, along with the need to inject more enthusiasm into it. *Moto Revue*'s leader spelled out the problem: '... marked by the slow agony of a formula which has had its hour of glory ...' and the proposed changes: '... next year's race will be run with two riders ... capacity classes recognised by the FIM ... production machines of which 50 had been made.' It was to be a very strict formula, extending even down to which parts could be changed at a pit stop.

1954 did see some changes; two riders were permitted, but were not obligatory and out of 39 solos, eight riders elected not to have a partner. Five sidecar outfits were entered and the outright winner was a 250 Puch which ran for 2,521 km compared with 2,438 km for the second-place 350 BSA. As for standard production machines, one of the more interesting models was a 175 Ydral with a half-fairing, faired-in seat hump and a kneeler riding position which clearly showed the open exhaust.

The next year a 350 works Jawa took the Bol, despite opposition from other works teams which also gave the appearance of a lot of factory support for the race. Things were certainly looking up with official riders from BMW, Jawa, Pannonia, Puch, Triumph, Zundapp. Other makes represented were FN, Norton, Matchless, Ariel, BSA, Horex, Maico, Alcyon, Peugeot, Automoto, Ydral, AGF, Motobécane, Morini, Guiller, Malterre and Lambretta. Yes, there was finally an official category for scooters and the organisers were beginning to differentiate between *série* (production) and *sport*

machines.

It came to a complicated head in 1956, with classes for *course* (racing), *sport* and *série* in 500, 350, 250, 175 motorcycles, 175 scooters, 350 sidecars (*série* only – just one entry) and 750 sidecars (*série* and *sport* – only three entries).

So from a total entry of 50, there were 18 class winners! What it did for those who had to keep track of the results is anybody's guess but there must be a lesson there for future race committees. Looking on the bright side, though, where else could you see a Manx Norton, a works Jawa, a standard Lambretta and a Royal Enfield combination race one another? The Lefèvre/Briand Manx Norton travelled 2,698 km, which was further than anyone else.

1957 saw an upsurge in the scooter class, while the sidecar entry was down to just three machines. The best-placed sidecar, a 750 Zundapp racing outfit, was eleventh and the best scooter, a 175 Rumi, also in racing trim, only managed 25th place overall.

Briand and Lefèvre once again took their Manx Norton to an overall win but the pure racers didn't have it all their own way. There were 26 bikes listed as racers, yet second place went to a production 500 BMW, and third place to a 500 Velocette in the sports category.

The fully faired Liberia-Ydral took the 175 class and came in fourth overall. This racer had a fully streamlined 'dustbin' fairing with a single headlamp unit neatly mounted in the nose. It averaged just over 100 km/h, which is not unimpressive for a 175 cc machine, compared with the race-winning average of 117·9 km/h set by the 500 Norton. The ultimate attraction of such a race was beginning to show through – there is an appealing paradox in racing a 175 against a 500, or a roadster against a racer. The simple power difference would make it a nonsense in a short circuit race, yet at the Bol d'Or the lightweights and the roadsters were easily holding their own. After the Ydral racer, the next *racing* solo was a 250 Adler in 15th place. With the exception of the sidecar in 11th position, the gap was filled by sports and production machines.

The essential point is that there was no real need for complicated classifications. Roadsters and racers were pretty evenly distributed at the start and there were roughly equal numbers in each capacity class although the 350s and 500s were slightly outnumbered by the 175s and 250s. Yet the overall results reflect no bias towards any particular group.

Using R, S and P to denote racer, sports or production, the final classification was:
1st – 500R; 2nd – 500P; 3rd – 500S; 4th – 175R; 5th – 250P; 6th – 250P; 7th – 350P; 8th – 250S; 9th — 350P; 10th – 250S.

Probably a more detailed analysis would show that the more experienced teams and those who were best prepared and best organised stood the most chance of winning, irrespective of the size or type of machine. Such an analysis might have shown the organisers the way to go. By grossly simplifying the class structure the event would have more appeal and it would concentrate its prize fund on overall winners and placings rather than spread it out over nearly 20 separate 'winners'.

Hindsight makes that a lot easier to say, because when the event was finally reorganised in the early '70s, that is precisely what happened.

But in 1957 there was no indication of what was to happen. Temporary booms in lightweights and scooters tended to hide the general depression facing the motorcycle industry. There were many factors involved, but the end result, after the attendance of works BMWs in 1959, was that only 31 starters lined up in 1960 and 10 teams finished. The lack of riders was matched only by the lack of spectators at the Montlhéry circuit. Only 800 people turned up and the balance sheet, to name but one aspect, was a disaster. The event was abandoned and virtually forgotten.

By the end of the '60s the Japanese manufacturers had dominated European sales; the trade was flourishing once more and the intense factory involvement in Grand Prix racing was fading away. *Moto Revue* were looking for a suitable national race to sponsor; the Bol d'Or was remembered and so the race was revived at Montlhéry in 1969.

The formula was simplified, with just two classes, up to 250 cc and over 250 cc. The division between production and modified machines was vague, to say the least but, from previous experience and the progress of other events such as the Barcelona 24-hour race which catered for 'prototypes', the distinction doesn't seem important.

The '69 race saw some semi-works machinery, including a Honda entered by Bill Smith which wasn't allowed to race because the riders did not have French national licences. Another, complete with factory mechanics, and entered by M. Villaseca (of Japauto), only arrived a few days before the race. It was obviously worth the effort because the machine won, ridden by Rougerie and Urdich.

The machine which came closest to being a racer was a TD2 Yamaha which had been detuned by having roadster cylinder barrels fitted. Its electrical power for lighting was supplied by a generator mounted on top of the gearbox, driven by belt from a pulley mounted on the gearbox sprocket. During the day the belt was removed.

This was the era of the superbikes — something which was to help elevate the Bol d'Or by providing the ideal type of machinery — quick enough to provide dramatic racing, reliable enough to last the distance, readily available and the subject of a new racing concept, F750.

The new Honda CB750 brought racer-like specifica-

tions into daily use, while the three-cylinder Tridents and Rocker 3s proved that the roadster could find a place on the race-track. Doug Hele's works Tridents were ideal for this type of racing and one ridden by Paul Smart and Tom Dickie won the 1970 Bol d'Or.

Factory support for events like the Daytona and Imola 200-mile races eventually meant that race kits became available for the big machines. Other concerns such as Ducati, Laverda, BMW and Guzzi found that the prototype class suited their needs, being able to modify existing machines or race real prototypes from which future roadsters would be produced.

The 1970 race had 250, 500 and over-500 classes and for the privateer there was a wide selection of machines such as the 500 Suzuki and Kawasaki, which gave varying combinations of speed and reliability. In fact the first 500 was a Suzuki ridden by Decombeix and Chemarin.

The result was an immediate success which satisfied riders, spectators and manufacturers. It hinged on the wide choice of machinery and the technical rivalry between modified production bikes and racers which needed de-tuning for reliability.

Because of this lack of rules, the Bol d'Or didn't meet the requirements of the newly-formed Coupe d'Endurance, the FIM's endurance-racing championship based on points awarded at selected long-distance races. But it is interesting to note that the Bol d'Or's emphasis shifted more and more towards prototype machines and that the FIM eventually changed their requirements in order to encompass the French race.

The racers were represented by a Sonauto TD2 Yamaha, with barrels from the roadster YDS6, and two H1R Kawasakis. But they made no impression on the big four-strokes; a 650 Triumph came second and the first ten places were filled by 750 cc four-strokes. Most of these machines fell into an 'intermediate' class, being basically roadsters fitted with race kits. The works Tridents had been timed at 226 km/h (141 mph) and the semi-official Hondas were reckoned to be quicker still. The first of the big-bore bikes appeared — the Japauto Honda which, with 70 mm pistons, displaced 950 cc.

The Montlhéry circuit could no longer accommodate the growing race and, in 1971, it was moved to the Bugatti circuit at Le Mans. The move had a lot to do with the future popularity of the event because Le Mans — the town as well as the circuit — is geared up to catering for this kind of race. As the excitement builds up during practice week, everything swings into a carnival, of which the race is only a part. The circuit features everything from camp-sites to motorcycle shows to discos. And with the crowds attracted to the big, fast bikes and the works-supported riders, the organisers weren't slow to take advantage of these built-in side-attractions.

Once again, the race went to Doug Hele's triple, this

time a BSA ridden by Tait and Pickrell. The endurance world was livening up and there were many different kinds of development. The big roadsters were obviously favoured; out of eight 750 Hondas, three were factory machines and the state of tune ranged from standard to Daytona specification. The Japauto had grown to 969 cc but still relied on a stock frame.

Moto Guzzi turned up with 850 cc works prototypes, with electric start and adjustable Koni dampers. Smaller bikes such as the Kawasaki triples had the performance and the teams were beginning to find the reliability — Eric Offenstadt's H1R was the first 500 and finished 5th overall. Not that sheer performance was the essential ingredient because the 500 BSA singles, sponsored by Mead and Tomkinson and ridden by Brown, Rollason, Heath, Gurner and Melody were getting quite a reputation in long-distance events. Based on the motocross engine, these machines gave around 36 hp but they often took the 500 class and finished well up in the overall placings. At Le Mans the Brown/Rollason machine came 8th overall. Other models were based on motocross engines, such as the 360 Bultaco which won outright at Barcelona in 1969.

At the completely-standard end of the scale, the Hungarian firm of Pannonia were tempted to return to the Bol d'Or and turned up with two roadster 250s. These bikes were *complete* roadsters, down to the valanced mudguards and fully enclosed chains. They had . .

Read in action on the 76 RCB in the '77 Bol d'Or
(photo by Rod Sloane)

The Bol d'Or

small single-leading-shoe brakes and were claimed to do 150 km/h (93 mph).

By 1972 there was less emphasis on class winners, only the *classement général* received any wide publicity. The other notable difference was that the endurance specialists were beginning to get their sums right and to make their presence felt. The race was won by Debrock and Ruiz on a 969 Japauto, now housed in a Dresda frame and weighing only 170 kg.

For the first time the Godier/Genoud team paired

together and finished second, riding a 750 Honda in an Egli frame. The Engli-Honda also weighed 170 kg and carried an 8-litre oil tank to avoid using an oil cooler and to do away with the need to top up at pit stops. It had other interesting features like cast alloy wheels and a four-into-one exhaust. The third team were also Honda mounted, on a semi-official machine entered by Alf Briggs.

The results, listing 23 finishers out of 60 starters, emphasised the need for specialist teams and machines designed to live through the stresses and crashes of a 24-hour event.

Bearing this in mind, the rain-soaked race in 1973 can be seen as a turning point. Official factory interest became a reality with plenty of Japanese putting in an appearance and the bikes suddenly became purpose-built for maximum *efficiency* both on the track and in the pits.

The Potoczny/Batesti Ducati is typical of the fleet of European models – BMW, Guzzi, Laverda, Ducati and even the odd Triumph – running in the wake of the Hondas and Kawasakis

(photo by John Robinson)

Another point worth noting is that the capacity classes finally disappeared.

In general, the bikes were changing to suit the event despite the high cost compared with running a production machine. Cast alloy wheels were appearing on more machines, as were disc brakes. Only one model relied on drums and most bikes were using discs at the rear, too. The most popular systems were Lockheed or the newly-available Brembo calipers, because on these types the pads were retained with clips or split pins and could therefore be changed very quickly.

An increasing number of machines had four, three or two into one exhausts. Ease of access and the minimum of crash damage was as important here as any performance gain and, with the wider, four-cylinder engines the simpler exhaust layout gave better ground clearance.

Twin headlamps, often faired into the streamlining, or powerful additional spotlamps helped the rider during the night, and to speed up refuelling stops aircraft type fillers were being fitted. The McLaren type used on one of the Yamahas could dump 27 litres in 5·5 seconds. This led to spillage problems on the pit road which – then and now – presented a hazard both from the fire risk and by making the ground slippery. Most 24-hour races see some incidents in the pits which are associated with spilt fuel and so far nothing serious has happened but neither has anything been done to reduce the risk.

The machines were also beginning to use QD components, like Dzus fasteners to mount fairings, etc., footrests and controls mounted on bolt-on plates and all the electrical components mounted on a board with a single, multi-pin connector. The reason was that these parts could be removed or changed as rapidly as possible if the components failed or were damaged in a crash. To speed pitwork further, the minimum number of bolt sizes were used around the bike, reducing the range of spanners needed and avoiding confusion when the mechanics had to work under pressure.

Preparation like this paid off well in the race. There were very few retirements due to mechanical failures – most were due to the wet and slippery conditions causing crashes, fuelling problems, electrical failures and so on. Drive chains were also suffering badly – a problem which was to become endemic.

This year, 1973, saw plenty of newcomers where the bikes themselves were concerned. Kawasaki's 903 cc Z1 was a prime candidate and ten were entered including official machines from the French importer SIDEMM which came complete with works mechanics and Yoshimura Junior. Claiming 96 bhp, these machines ran on 31 mm carburetters, Yoshimura cams and drove through a close-ratio gearbox. They used SMAC wheels with K81 Dunlops and carried Cibié lights.

Yamaha were also represented by three of the ill-fated 750 balance-shaft four-strokes. Fitted with works

engines they boasted modified pistons, cams, carburetters and exhausts. One had gearbox trouble, one had problems with the balance shaft and the third broke its cam chain. A privately entered two-stroke fared rather better. The Bourgeois/Jimenez TZ350, prepared by Maingret and powering its lights via a total loss system, finished 11th.

The official Suzuki-Europe race team turned up with two 750 triples in Daytona trim, albeit detuned slightly, 'to preserve the tyres and chains'. Both bikes suffered crank failures during the night.

Works support also came from England, this time in the form of the John Player Norton of Peter Williams and Dave Croxford. This was the year of the short-stroke motor slung in a monocoque frame and it was accompanied by the more orthodox Norvil production racer to be ridden by Butcher and Scully. An unfortunate incident during practice left the number one bike burnt out after a backfire and the riders took over the long-stroke production machine. Unfortunately this dropped out, six hours into the race.

Honda were there in force, with fourteen machines; the 969 cc Japauto, an 820, an 810, eight 750s (three of which had works engines) and three 500 fours. Most were eliminated or set well down the field by crashes but the Japauto won the race, covering 2,764 km. The 750s, with the racing kit, were not unlike the Daytona models except that they had a less violent cam. The frames were replicas of the Daytona model, built in the UK from factory drawings.

BMW made their official return to solo racing with two of their new 900 motors fitted with 38 mm Dell 'Orto carburetters and producing a claimed 84 hp. The engine was lifted some 30 mm in the frame to give ground clearance, the suspension modified and the bikes lightened extensively, weighing only 180 kg compared to 218 kg for the roadster. The machine ridden by Dahne and Green came in third but the other, entered by Gus Kuhn and ridden by Potter and Sharpe crashed after 12 hours.

With such a level of works support the day of machines like the 500 BSA was rapidly coming to a close. Nevertheless, one ridden by Brown/Gurner finished in 22nd place after they had changed a piston in 45 minutes. Another model, ridden by Bowler/Knight, had a drum front brake with hydraulic operation to give automatic adjustment.

The factories were interested and taking the event seriously; Japauto had asserted their position as specialists but there were five Kawasakis in the first seven places ...

The increase in machine performance was by this time showing weaknesses in the tyres and transmissions. As is so often the case, new developments were only just around the corner and for 1974 the racers had a choice of 'wet' or 'dry' tyres, which made life a bit easier for the riders and even more hectic for the team managers. They now had to forecast the weather in addition to their other duties. A direct development from this situation was that bikes appeared with QD wheels.

The heavy machines also had handling problems and the entry list featured many special frames to house the big engines. Mead and Tomkinson had switched to a bigger power unit, the three cylinder Laverda, which was built into a frame with Difazio front suspension and hub-centre steering. This machine also had a hydraulically operated clutch using a brake master cylinder which had to work upside down as it was on the left handlebar, and needed a fluid supply from a remote reservoir.

Many of the machines had used longer levers to reduce the rider's effort during braking but now there were new variations. The official Kawasaki ridden by Léon/Duhamel had one front disc linked with the rear disc, both being operated by the foot control, while the handlebar level operated the second front disc.

Japauto, in an effort to reduce pad changes, had a twin disc set-up with four calipers, one behind and one in front of each fork leg.

More thought was going into general chassis design and, in addition to the frame kits, many bikes had fairings which enveloped the rider and gave maximum weather protection. The humped racing seats were becoming quite useful, too. The Kawasaki-Kings seat contained a reserve fuel tank, tools and a spare chain.

But '74 was the year of Godier and Genoud. Now with a Kawasaki in their Egli frame they won the Bol d'Or, covering 2,877 km, after winning the Barcelona 24-hour, the 1,000 km race at Mettet and coming second at the Spa 24-hour race. It wasn't easy, though. After seven hours of racing the Godier/Genoud machine was on the same lap as the Kawasaki of Léon and Duhamel. Both eventually stopped to sort out minor problems and let Luc/Rigal through on the BMW. Using racing tyres, the Kawasakis were making up ground until the BM's motor blew two hours from the end leaving Godier/Genoud to take the flag followed by the Kawasaki ridden by Guili/Choukron and the Debrock/Chemarin Honda 860.

The big fours were dominating the results – the first European bike was the seventh-placed Guzzi 850 and the real racers weren't doing so well either. This year a Yamaha TZ700 had been entered but was abandoned half-way through.

The following year a more serious attempt was made by Boinet/Debrock with another TZ700. They set the fastest practice time and lef from the start of the race. A broken chain, costing them a few places, was the only major incident and they brought the watercooled Yamaha into 6th place. The 350 Yamaha-powered SMAC ridden by Offenstadt/Coq was 7th. The big Kawasakis were unbeatable, though, and scored a

1–2–3, followed by the BMW 980 of Dahne and Guili and yet another Kawasaki.

The official team Kawasakis, expressly built for this kind of racing, had the most extensive back-up so far seen in endurance and some of the most experienced riders. During the early stages, when they were chasing the TZ Yamaha, Duhamel crashed one of the big fours. His partner, Baldé, took over and also crashed. Godier and Genoud had got in front of the Yamaha and the only other make in the running was the Ferrari/Grau works Ducati. This leading bunch were lapping consistently around the 1 m 54 mark. The Duhamel/Baldé machine, down in 44th place after repair work had been done, proceeded to make up time, lapping at 1 m 55 through the night! The leading Kawasaki had eased off to 2 m 01 and, when it rained at 4 am and most bikes slowed to 2 m 30 or more, the Kawasakis kept on at 2 m 20. By day-light, Duhamel and Baldé were in 6th place, having made up this ground in conditions so bad that 26 teams had dropped out during the night. They eventually finished third.

Other teams were emulating the approach made by the SIDEMM Kawasakis, using big, four-cylinder engines in special frames such as PEM (Japauto), Rickman, Segoni, Dresda, Egli, Intermeca and so on. But Godier managed to stay one jump ahead and the team Kawasakis not only had special frames for handling and lightness – they were built specifically for this type of race. To this end they featured QD components and gave rapid access to the mechanical parts.

The engines themselves were only mildly tuned, being taken out to the 1000 cc limit, using some Yoshimura components, 31 mm Keihin carburetters and four-into-one Devil exhausts.

Honda were using two types of engine at this time; one was a 900 based on the CB750 and the other was a new 750 based on the 500-four. This had its camshaft driven by gears instead of a chain but wasn't very successful.

1976 was probably the peak year for the Bol d'Or, with maximum support from the public, competitors and factories. It was also the year when Honda made a serious attack on the Coupe d'Endurance with their RCB750s. These were still similar in appearance to the prototypes built by Honda's RSC for 1975. The designation RCB750 refers not to the engine size but to the design which was based on the bottom half of the CB750 roadster. Unfortunately, just as Honda were building up to their climax, the Kawasakis had reached the end of their development. With no direct support from the Japanese factory, Godier said they could do little more and certainly couldn't compete with the highly-organised teams from Honda. That didn't stop the Kawasakis from sharing the first six places pretty evenly with Honda, though. Honda France won with Chemarin, and Alex

George stepping in for the injured Christian Léon. The Sarron/Boulom and Duhamel/Baldé Kawasakis were second and third followed by Stan Woods and Jack Findlay on the Honda Britain machine. Honda also took fifth place and Kawasaki was sixth. The first bike which wasn't a Japanese four was a 1000 cc Guzzi, in fifteenth place.

Probably the most impressive thing about the race was the vast array of individual designs and innovations. This was brought about partly by the need to keep up with the leading teams, partly to make the readily-available engines suitable and partly to make sure the machine could keep up the pace and stay intact. Tyre developments and newly available damper units had brought radical changes in suspension and roadholding — if the chassis could make use of them. Increased power from the bigger engines plus the ability to use power for

more of the time had also had a deleterious effect on chains.

The ideas started by the Godier team had caught on and there were many attempts to use the chassis in order to improve the machine as a whole. These were as varied as the machines themselves.

Starting at the racer end of the spectrum, there were three Yamahas entered, two 350s — one in the unusual Offenstadt chassis — and a TZ750. The big two-stroke, ridden by Evans and Boinet, was easily the fastest machine on the circuit. It led the field from the start but

Honda CBX in the Bol d'Argent production race. Like some of the endurance machines, this one is fitted with radio

(photo by John Robinson)

The Bol d'Or

ironically it didn't even pick up the prizes awarded to the leading bike at the end of each hour. The reason was the frequency of the Yamaha's pit stops. Its high fuel consumption, plus a fault which entailed changing the brake pads four times in three hours, meant that it was in the pits as each hour drew to a close. It was stopping once every 40 minutes, compared to the 1h 20m stints of the Hondas. The effect of this — and the bike's pace once it was going — can be seen by its placing at the end of each hour. From its early lead it could manage only 4th place at the end of the first hour, then 11th, 8th and 6th before dropping to 9th. From there it slid down the field, suffer-

Ron Pierce on the Yoshimura Suzuki which he shared with Wes Cooley

(photo by Dave Walker)

ing fractured exhausts before it finally retired at 3 am, its chain jammed around the gearbox sprocket.

One of the 350s only lasted four hours before its pistons failed, but the machine shared by Offenstadt and Gomis kept going — just — until the 23rd hour. This machine featured a highly unorthodox chassis with front suspension reminiscent of the old girder forks. The wheel was carried on a trailing link from which there was a strut to compress the spring unit carried in front of the steering head.

During the race the bike was plagued with electrical problems, circulating at one stage during the night with no lights at all. Its progress could be charted by the piercing screech of the exhaust amid the thunder of the four-strokes.

The RCBs which had been winning everything that year, weren't the only Hondas at the track. There was a

virtually standard 550-four entered by a Brazilian team which circulated steadily but reliably enough to finish 12th. There were the CB750 variants fielded by Japauto and Dholda, distinguished mainly by their chassis parts. The latter, entered by the Belgian dealer d'Hollander, had a heavily triangulated frame which went around the engine rather than over it and which carried a four-bar rear suspension. This kind of linkage gives more control over wheel movement, allowing it, for example, to keep constant chain tension.

The Japautos boasted enormous fairings which literally dwarfed the riders. Their PEM frames featured swinging arms which were triangulated, with a secondary loop under the main fork. This assembly proved so rigid that one of the machines used only one damper, an adjustable de Carbon unit. This machine was ridden by Gary Green and Dave Croxford who, from the anticipated winnings, had promised to buy Japauto a matching damper for the other side. Their normal power units were over-bored CB750s, as fitted to the second machine ridden by Degens and Sailler, but Honda France, having a spare RCB unit, let Japauto fit the engine to Croxford's machine. It finished 9th, after crashing heavily enough to wipe out the beautiful fairing (but without damaging the suspension).

Two other unusual Hondas appeared that year. Honda Suisse had fitted very neat frames around basically standard Gold Wing engines. The machines *looked* sleek and very small compared to the tall, in-line fours but, at 230 kg, they were still very heavy. Neither of them finished the race, although they did get results at other endurance events. A later venture with a Gold Wing in the UK proved that the three-bearing crank was unsuitable for racing purposes.

European machines were represented by Ducati, BMW, Moto-Guzzi – including one of the automatics – and Laverda. Most of these machines were in relatively standard trim, the notable exception being Mead and Tomkinson's entry. Using the 980 cc Laverda triple, the machine was hub-centre steered and, like the Belgian Dholda, had a type of parallelogram rear suspension. In this system the conventional swinging arm is replaced by two radius arms. The position of the pivot points and the lengths of the two arms control the vertical movement of the wheel. One advantage of such an arrangement is constant chain tension and, theoretically, the chassis should give rigidity in the planes where it is needed and maximum control over steering and suspension movement combined with light weight. Complete with a fairing which is best described as comprehensive, the Laverda was, in fact, very heavy. It weighed in at 220 kg, compared with, say 167 kg for the Godier-Genoud machine.

The chain wear problem was beginning to get serious and there were a number of moves to counter it (the heavy-duty chains are all-riveted, so removal and replace-ment is time-consuming, while the prospect of a worn chain breaking or jumping the sprocket and getting jammed is even less appealing). While some bikes had suspension designed to make the chain's life easier, others reinforced the chain itself. One Ducati had a duplex rear chain. Honda, with a vested interest in both winning races and in roadster reliability, produced a new chain for the 76 RCB. Within a year this 'long-life' chain would be used on their roadsters.

The level of speed and competition which endurance racing had reached was not unimpressive. These giant machines lapped the Le Mans Bugatti circuit within a couple of seconds of Lucchinelli's lap record set at the French GP. The winning Honda covered 3,235 km and, after 24 hours of racing, the Sarron/Boulom Kawasaki was only 3 km behind.

For 1977 Honda had up-dated the RCB and there were various official and semi-official teams equipped with both 76 and 77 models. These included entries from France, and Britain under the HERT banner, plus teams from Belgium, Germany, Switzerland and Holland. With no factory support for the Kawasakis and no other manufacturer in a position to challenge Honda, this led to a complete domination of the endurance series. This was what Honda had set out to do and they won the *Coupe d'Endurance* three years in a row, '76, '77 and '78. One can only admire this remarkable performance and praise the outstanding performance of the various RCB models but it was removing the innovation and the driving force which had made endurance racing so fascinating. Where teams like Japauto, Dholda and Honda Suisse once had to build their own machines in their own ways, it was now much easier to accept the RCB and use it. In achieving the most unlikely feat of being able to supply an over-the-counter endurance racer, Honda had made an amazing contribution to the sport and at the same time detracted from the very essence of endurance racing. If they were to make RCB's available it would probably have much the same effect as the Gold Star in clubman's racing or the Manx and later TZ Yamaha in GP racing. Everyone who wanted to be competitive would have to buy one and the races would turn into repetitive processions.

The '78 race, not surprisingly, featured works Hondas in first, second and third places. The general level of machine innovations was down on previous years, although there were more racers entered than before. One of these, a specially prepared Sonauto OW31 Yamaha, caused most of the excitement. Ridden by Pons and Sarron it set fastest practice time and shot into the lead as the race started. Despite the fragility of the two-stroke, the frequency of fuelling stops and the total-loss lighting, which involved changing the battery at every pit stop, it stayed in the lead for nearly 18 hours before its crankshaft failed. There is an incentive for this kind of

The Bol d'Or

performance, namely 1,000F for every hour the bike stays in front, plus an additional 5,000F for the best performance in any one hour.

Several other entries were new to endurance racing, including the Laverda V-6, making its first public appearance, a Yoshimura-prepared Suzuki GS, two shaft-drive 1100 cc Yamahas and a CBX Honda with a factory-prepared engine. With machinery like this and the right kind of development, even the RCB will be hard-pressed to stay supreme.

1978 saw two new twists to the Bol d'Or story. The Le Mans circuit, where the Bol had re-grown to world-wide fame, staged a separate 24-hour race. This was not included in the *Coupe d'Endurance,* and operated two machine categories, prototypes and silhouettes, which had to conform to homologation type regulations. The

Bol d'Or itself moved to the Paul Ricard circuit in southern France. Increasing the span of the carnival atmosphere which *is* the Bol d'Or, the organisers ran the traditional Coupe Kawasaki and Challenge Honda supporting races, plus 250 and 750 National Championships and a six-hour production race, the Bol d'Argent. This ran through to midnight Friday, preceding Saturday's 4 pm start to the Bol d'Or. Including practice, the organisers were able to offer a four-day festival of racing backed up by a host of side attractions.

These new turns, plus the FIM's proposed World Championship status for endurance racing, bring the Bol d'Or to yet another cross-roads. The decision to change with the new generations of roadsters, to conform with the FIM or to go their own way, rests with the organisers of the Bol d'Or. And that decision may determine the future of endurance racing, with any number of possibilities ranging from a longer-than-average production race to the exciting free-for-all racing of the past.

The End – Le Mans style
(photo by Motorcycle Mechanics)

Bol d'Or results 1922 to 1978

Year	Circuit	Winner's Distance (km)	Overall positions – rider (machine)		
			First	**Second**	**Third**
1922	Vaujours	1,245	Zind (500 Motosacoche)	Naas (500 Gnôme et Rhône)	Clech (250 Motosolo)
1923	St Germain	1,404	Zind (500 Motosacoche)	Pinney (500 Triumph)	Lambert (500) *
1924	"	1,535	Francisquet (500 Sunbeam)	Hufkens (350 Gillet)	Reinartz (350 Gillet)
1925	"	1,616	Francisquet (500 Sunbeam)	Damitio (500 Sunbeam)	Dupont (175 DFR)
1926	"	1,627	Damitio (500 Sunbeam)	Bernard (500 Gnôme et Rhône)	Andreino (500 Norton)
1927	Fontainebleau	1,698	Lempereur (350 FN)	Debaissieux (500 Monet-Goyon)	**
1928	St Germain	1,521	Vroonen (500 Gillet-Herstal)	Fournier (350 Roléo)	Roudadoux (250 Dé-Dé)
1929	"	1,763	Vroonen (500 Gillet-Herstal)	James (500 Rudge Whitworth)	Bernard (500 Gnôme et Rhône)
1930	"	1,826	Debaissieux (500 Monet-Goyon)	Caron (500 Gillet-Herstal)	Patural (350 Velocette)
1931	"	1,872	Patural (350 Velocette)	Perrin (350 Jonghi)	Jeannin (350 Jonghi)
1932	"	1,885	Jeannin (350 Jonghi)	Patural (350 Velocette)	Lovenfosse (500 Motobécane)
1933	"	1,952	Boura (350 Velocette)	Lovenfosse (500 Motobécane)	Henry (350 Motobécane)
1934	"	2,031	Willing (350 Velocette)	Narcy (500 Peugeot)	Richy (350) *
1935	"	2,056	Boura (350 Norton)	Patuelli (350 Velocette)	Fouret (350) *
1936	"	2,068	Craet (500 Gillet-Herstal)	Tessari (350 Velocette)	Hufkens (500 Gillet-Herstal)
1937	Montlhéry	1,889	Tabard (500 Norton)	Poinot (250 Motobécane)	Lefèvre (500) *
1938	"	2,004	Tinoco (1000 Harley-Davidson – Bernadet sidecar)	LeRoy (250 Terrot)	Francoise (600 Motobécane – Bernadet sidecar)

Bol d'Or results 1922 to 1978

Year	Circuit	Winner's Distance (km)	Overall positions – rider (machine)		
			First	**Second**	**Third**
1939	Montlhéry	1,951	Hordelalay (600 Motobécane – Bernadet sidecar)	Beauvais (600 Motobécane – Bernadet sidecar)	Venin (500 Saroléa)
1940–1946 no race held					
1947	St Germain	2,057	Lefèvre (500 Norton)	L'Heritier (500 Norton)	Ladeveze (500 Ariel)
1948	"	1,900	J. Lenglet (500 BMW)	R. Lenglet (500 BMW)	Betemps (BMW sidecar)
1949	Montlhéry	2,384	Lefèvre (500 Norton)	Laver (500 Norton)	Massiot (500 BMW)
1950	"	2,432	Lefèvre (500 Norton)	Juigne (350 Douglas)	Herve (350 Jawa)
1951	St Germain	2,343	Lefèvre (500 Norton)	Weingartmann (250 Puch)	Moury (250 Puch)
1952	Montlhéry	2,332	Colligon (250 Guzzi)	Weingartmann (250 Puch)	Moury (250 Puch)
1953	"	2,573	Lefèvre (500 Norton)	Weingartmann (250 Puch)	Bonte (500 CEMEC)
1954	"	2,521	Weingartman/Volzwinkler (250 Puch)	Rossignol/Goil (350 BSA)	Piel/Dore (500 CEMEC)
1955	"	2,410	Harsmid/Klimt (350 Jawa)	Lefèvre/Briand (500 Norton)	Kania/Beauvais (500 Horex)
1956	"	2,698	Lefèvre/Briand (500 Norton)	Klimt/Harsmid (350 Jawa)	Galland/Gillet (500 Triumph)
1957	"	2,830	Lefèvre/Briand (500 Norton)	Nenning/Weissgerber (500 BMW)	Tano/Cherrier (500 Velocette)
1958	"	2,626	Inizan/Mutel (500 Triumph)	Nenning/Delaherche (500 BMW)	Bernard/Bergeron 350 DKW)
1959	"	2,962	Briand/Bargetzi (500 Norton)	Furling/Merle (500 BMW)	Inizan/Mutel (500 Triumph)
1960	"	2,733	Vasseur/Maucherat (500 BMW)	Bargetzi/Mantear (500 BMW)	Michaux/Bono (350 Peugeot)
1961–1968 race not held					
1969	Montlhéry	2,796	Rougerie/Urdich (750 Honda)	Evenard/Morel (500 Kawasaki)	Huguet/Danzer (500 Kawasaki)
1970	"	2,947	Dickie/Smart (750 Triumph)	Darvill/Chevalier (650 Triumph/Rickman)	Angiolini/Brettoni (750 Laverda)
1971	Le Mans	2,727	Pickrell/Tait (750 BSA)	Brettoni/Cretti (750 Laverda)	Brambilla/Mandracci (850 Guzzi)
1972	"	2,896	Debrock/Ruiz (950 Japauto Honda)	Godier/Genoud (750 Honda)	Williams/Woods (750 Honda)
1973	"	2,764	Debrock/Tchernine (969 Japauto)	Renouf/Guili (903 Kawa-Kings)	Dahne/Green (899 BMW)

Year	Circuit	Winner's Distance (km)	Overall positions – rider (machine)		
			First	**Second**	**Third**
1974	Le Mans	2,877	Godier/Genoud (903 Egli-Kawasaki)	Guili/Choukron (1000 Kawasaki)	Debrock/Chemarin (860 Honda)
1975	"	2,988	Godier/Genoud (1000 Kawasaki)	Estrosi/Husson (986 Kawasaki)	Duhamel/Baldé (1000 Kawasaki)
1976	"	3,231	Chemarin/George (941 Honda)	Sarron/Boulom (1000 Kawasaki)	Duhamel/Baldé (1000 Kawasaki)
1977	"	3,235	Léon/Chemarin (997 Honda)	Frutschi/Baldé (1000 Kawasaki)	Huguet/Korhonen (997 Honda)
1978	Paul Ricard	3,503	Léon/Chemarin (1000 Honda)	Luc/Rigal (1000 Honda)	Woods/Williams (1000 Honda)

Note : * *amateur riders often entered in the name of their club, without specifying the make of machine.*

** *because the race was run in several capacity classes at this time, it is not always possible to calculate overall positions.*

Printed by
Haynes Publishing Group
Sparkford Yeovil Somerset
England